This PILOT'S
LOGBOOK

↘ *For Simmers*

── BELONGS TO ──

....

....

....

My PC Specs

For my SIM GAME

☐ FSX ☐ FS2020 ☐ X-PLANE ☐ OTHER

MOTHERBOARD:

CHIPSET:

CPU:

MEMORY (DRAM):

GRAPHIC CARD:

GRAPHIC CARD MEMORY:

HARD DISK DRIVE 1:

HARD DISK DRIVE 2:

POWER SUPPLY / COOLING:

VR DEVICE:

OTHER:

THANK YOU FOR BUYING THIS BOOK!

Our "**Pilot Logbook for Simmers**" isn't just another "flight planner" layout *"copied & pasted"* you can find everywhere. Many times copied but here is the genuine one. It was designed by **REAL a**viation enthusiasts and flight simulation true fans.

This handy Notebook is made specifically for "**Flight Simmers**", who need to take notes and jotting down all the information needed during preflight planning or while en-route flight, ... and you know there is quite a lot of information there!

We have created this PILOT LOGBOOK COLLECTION of notebooks with love and great care, just FOR YOU guys!

And yes, mistakes can always happen!
For any quality issues with this book such as faulty binding, or printing errors, etc. please do not hesitate to drop us an email at:
wohoofactory@gmail.com

Scan this code and follow us on Amazon!

DISCLAIMER:

This content is intended for flight simulation and home flight simulator enthusiasts only. It does not reflect or represent any real flight procedures and applications.

PLEASE DO NOT USE FOR REAL FLIGHTS

DATE: _____

FLIGHT INFORMATIONS

FROM		TO		**VFR**		**IFR**	
ACRFT. TYPE		ACRFT. ID / FLT #	____ I ____	☐		☐	
ETE *(Est. Flight Time)*		DEPART. TIME *(Zulu)*					

ROUTE / WAYPOINTS		**WIND**	**WX**
>			
>	____ / ____		
>			

DEPARTURE

GATE / RUNWAY		PAYLOAD		**ATC INSTRUCTIONS**
ALTIMETER		RESERVE		>
CLIMB RATE		QNH		>
TRANS ALT		SID		>
ZFW		SQUAWK		>
TOW		ATIS INFO		>
BLOCK FUEL		>		>
TAXIWAYS > RNW				>

TAKE OFF / CLIMB / CRUISE PHASE

V_1:		V_R:		V_2:

EST. TOP OF CLIMB	**ATC ACTUAL TOP OF CLIMB**
>	>

EST. CRUISE FLIGHT LEVEL	**ATC ACTUAL CRUISE FLIGHT LEVEL**
>	>

DESCENT PHASE / APPROACH

TOP OF DESCENT	TRANSITION ALTITUDE
>	>

STAR		FIELD ELEVATION		*Remarks*
QNH		MAG / WIND		>
ATIS INFO				

GO AROUND *(ALT / HDG / WAYPOINT)*	>	

RNW / GATE		V_{APP} *(Approach Speed)* :	V_{REF} *(Landing Speed)* :
TAXIWAYS > GATE		>	>

DEPARTURE ⌄		**COMMS**	**ARRIVAL** ⌄	
		REMARKS / NOTES		
GROUND			GROUND	
TOWER			TOWER	
CLEARANCE			APPROACH	
CONTROL			CONTROL	
RADAR			ILS	
ATIS / INFO			ATIS / INFO	
VATSIM			VATSIM	
IVAO			IVAO	

ADDITIONAL INFORMATION

SKECTCH

NOTES

DATE: _____

FLIGHT INFORMATIONS

FROM		TO		VFR	☐	IFR	☐
ACRFT. TYPE		ACRFT. ID / FLT #	_____ I _____				
ETE (Est. Flight Time)		DEPART. TIME (Zulu)					

ROUTE / WAYPOINTS		WIND	WX
>			
>		____ / ____	
>			

DEPARTURE

GATE / RUNWAY		PAYLOAD		ATC INSTRUCTIONS	
ALTIMETER		RESERVE		>	
CLIMB RATE		QNH		>	
TRANS ALT		SID		>	
ZFW		SQUAWK		>	
TOW		ATIS INFO		>	
BLOCK FUEL		>		>	
TAXIWAYS > RNW				>	

TAKE OFF / CLIMB / CRUISE PHASE

V_1:		V_R:		V_2:	

EST. TOP OF CLIMB	ATC ACTUAL TOP OF CLIMB
>	>

EST. CRUISE FLIGHT LEVEL	ATC ACTUAL CRUISE FLIGHT LEVEL
>	>

DESCENT PHASE / APPROACH

TOP OF DESCENT	TRANSITION ALTITUDE
>	>

STAR		FIELD ELEVATION		Remarks	
QNH		MAG / WIND		>	
ATIS INFO					

GO AROUND (ALT / HDG / WAYPOINT)	>		

RNW / GATE		V_{APP} (Approach Speed):	V_{REF} (Landing Speed):
TAXIWAYS > GATE		>	>

DEPARTURE ⌄		COMMS	ARRIVAL ⌄	
		REMARKS / NOTES		
GROUND			GROUND	
TOWER			TOWER	
CLEARANCE			APPROACH	
CONTROL			CONTROL	
RADAR			ILS	
ATIS / INFO			ATIS / INFO	
VATSIM			VATSIM	
IVAO			IVAO	

ADDITIONAL INFORMATION

SKECTCH

NOTES

DATE: _____

FLIGHT INFORMATIONS

FROM		TO		**VFR**	**IFR**
ACRFT. TYPE		ACRFT. ID / FLT #	_____ I _____	☐	☐
ETE *(Est. Flight Time)*		DEPART. TIME *(Zulu)*			

ROUTE / WAYPOINTS	**WIND**	**WX**
> > >	_____ / ____	

DEPARTURE

				ATC INSTRUCTIONS
GATE / RUNWAY		PAYLOAD		>
ALTIMETER		RESERVE		>
CLIMB RATE		QNH		>
TRANS ALT		SID		>
ZFW		SQUAWK		>
TOW		ATIS INFO		>
BLOCK FUEL		>		>
TAXIWAYS > RNW				>

TAKE OFF / CLIMB / CRUISE PHASE

V_1:	V_R:	V_2:

EST. TOP OF CLIMB	ATC ACTUAL TOP OF CLIMB
>	>

EST. CRUISE FLIGHT LEVEL	ATC ACTUAL CRUISE FLIGHT LEVEL
>	>

DESCENT PHASE / APPROACH

TOP OF DESCENT	TRANSITION ALTITUDE
>	>

STAR		FIELD ELEVATION		*Remarks*
QNH		MAG / WIND		>
ATIS INFO				

GO AROUND *(ALT / HDG / WAYPOINT)*	>	

RNW / GATE		V_{APP} *(Approach Speed)* :	V_{REF} *(Landing Speed)* :
TAXIWAYS > GATE		>	>

DEPARTURE ⌄		COMMS	ARRIVAL ⌄	
GROUND		**REMARKS / NOTES**	GROUND	
TOWER			TOWER	
CLEARANCE			APPROACH	
CONTROL			CONTROL	
RADAR			ILS	
ATIS / INFO			ATIS / INFO	
VATSIM			VATSIM	
IVAO			IVAO	

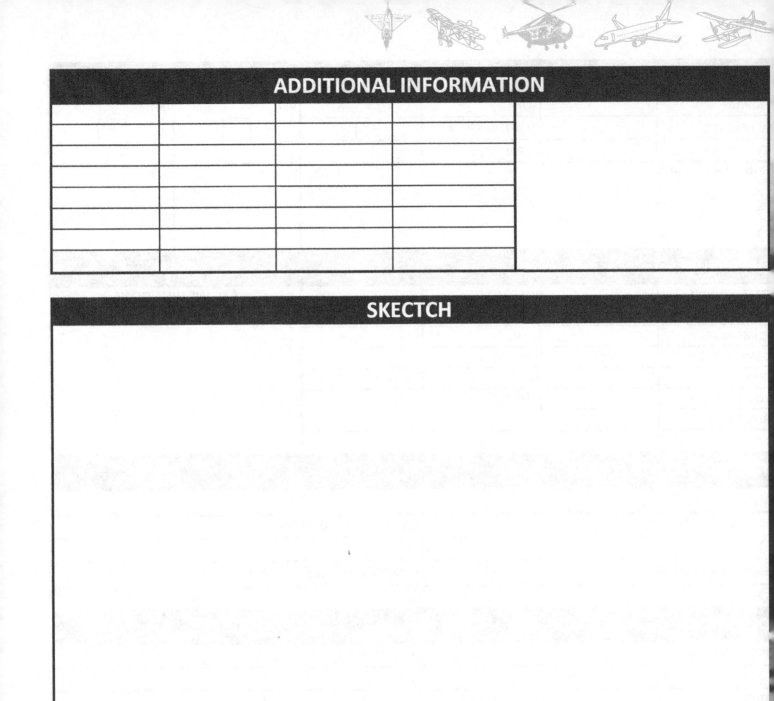

ADDITIONAL INFORMATION

SKECTCH

NOTES

DATE: _____

FLIGHT INFORMATIONS

FROM		TO			**VFR** ☐	**IFR** ☐
ACRFT. TYPE		ACRFT. ID / FLT #	_____ I _____			
ETE *(Est. Flight Time)*		DEPART. TIME *(Zulu)*				

ROUTE / WAYPOINTS		**WIND**	**WX**
>			
>		____ / ____	
>			

DEPARTURE

GATE / RUNWAY		PAYLOAD		**ATC INSTRUCTIONS**	
ALTIMETER		RESERVE		>	
CLIMB RATE		QNH		>	
TRANS ALT		SID		>	
ZFW		SQUAWK		>	
TOW		ATIS INFO		>	
BLOCK FUEL		>		>	
TAXIWAYS > RNW				>	

TAKE OFF / CLIMB / CRUISE PHASE

V_1:	V_R:	V_2:

EST. TOP OF CLIMB	ATC ACTUAL TOP OF CLIMB
>	>
EST. CRUISE FLIGHT LEVEL	ATC ACTUAL CRUISE FLIGHT LEVEL
>	>

DESCENT PHASE / APPROACH

TOP OF DESCENT	TRANSITION ALTITUDE
>	>

STAR		FIELD ELEVATION		*Remarks*
QNH		MAG / WIND		>
ATIS INFO				

GO AROUND *(ALT / HDG / WAYPOINT)*	>	

RNW / GATE		V_{APP} *(Approach Speed)* :	V_{REF} *(Landing Speed)* :
TAXIWAYS > GATE		>	>

DEPARTURE ⌄	COMMS	ARRIVAL ⌄
	REMARKS / NOTES	

DEPARTURE			ARRIVAL	
GROUND			GROUND	
TOWER			TOWER	
CLEARANCE			APPROACH	
CONTROL			CONTROL	
RADAR			ILS	
ATIS / INFO			ATIS / INFO	
VATSIM			VATSIM	
IVAO			IVAO	

ADDITIONAL INFORMATION

SKECTCH

NOTES

DATE: _____

FLIGHT INFORMATIONS

FROM		TO		VFR ☐	IFR ☐
ACRFT. TYPE		ACRFT. ID / FLT #	_____ I _____		
ETE *(Est. Flight Time)*		DEPART. TIME *(Zulu)*			

ROUTE / WAYPOINTS 🗺️	WIND ___ / ___	WX ☀️⛅☁️🌧️⛈️
>		
>		
>		

DEPARTURE

GATE / RUNWAY		PAYLOAD		ATC INSTRUCTIONS
ALTIMETER		RESERVE		>
CLIMB RATE		QNH		>
TRANS ALT		SID		>
ZFW		SQUAWK		>
TOW		ATIS INFO		>
BLOCK FUEL		>		>
TAXIWAYS > RNW				>

TAKE OFF / CLIMB / CRUISE PHASE

V_1:	V_R:	V_2:

EST. TOP OF CLIMB	ATC ACTUAL TOP OF CLIMB
>	>

EST. CRUISE FLIGHT LEVEL	ATC ACTUAL CRUISE FLIGHT LEVEL
>	>

DESCENT PHASE / APPROACH

TOP OF DESCENT	TRANSITION ALTITUDE
>	>

STAR		FIELD ELEVATION		Remarks
QNH		MAG / WIND		>
ATIS INFO				

GO AROUND *(ALT / HDG / WAYPOINT)* >	

RNW / GATE		V_{APP} *(Approach Speed)* :	V_{REF} *(Landing Speed)* :
TAXIWAYS > GATE		>	>

DEPARTURE 📡 ⌄	COMMS	ARRIVAL 📡 ⌄

		REMARKS / NOTES		
GROUND			GROUND	
TOWER			TOWER	
CLEARANCE			APPROACH	
CONTROL			CONTROL	
RADAR			ILS	
ATIS / INFO			ATIS / INFO	
VATSIM			VATSIM	
IVAO			IVAO	

ADDITIONAL INFORMATION

SKECTCH

NOTES

DATE: _____

FLIGHT INFORMATIONS

FROM		TO		**VFR**		**IFR**	
ACRFT. TYPE		ACRFT. ID / FLT #	_____ I _____	☐		☐	
ETE *(Est. Flight Time)*		DEPART. TIME *(Zulu)*					

ROUTE / WAYPOINTS	**WIND**	**WX**
> > >	_____ / _____	

DEPARTURE

GATE / RUNWAY		PAYLOAD		**ATC INSTRUCTIONS**
ALTIMETER		RESERVE		>
CLIMB RATE		QNH		>
TRANS ALT		SID		>
ZFW		SQUAWK		>
TOW		ATIS INFO		>
BLOCK FUEL		>		>
TAXIWAYS > RNW				>

TAKE OFF / CLIMB / CRUISE PHASE

V_1:	V_R:	V_2:

EST. TOP OF CLIMB	ATC ACTUAL TOP OF CLIMB
>	>

EST. CRUISE FLIGHT LEVEL	ATC ACTUAL CRUISE FLIGHT LEVEL
>	>

DESCENT PHASE / APPROACH

TOP OF DESCENT	TRANSITION ALTITUDE
>	>

STAR		FIELD ELEVATION		*Remarks*
QNH		MAG / WIND		>
ATIS INFO				

GO AROUND *(ALT / HDG / WAYPOINT)*	>	

RNW / GATE		V_{APP} *(Approach Speed)* :	V_{REF} *(Landing Speed)* :
TAXIWAYS > GATE		>	>

DEPARTURE	∨	**COMMS**	*ARRIVAL*	∨
GROUND		**REMARKS / NOTES**	GROUND	
TOWER			TOWER	
CLEARANCE			APPROACH	
CONTROL			CONTROL	
RADAR			ILS	
ATIS / INFO			ATIS / INFO	
VATSIM			VATSIM	
IVAO			IVAO	

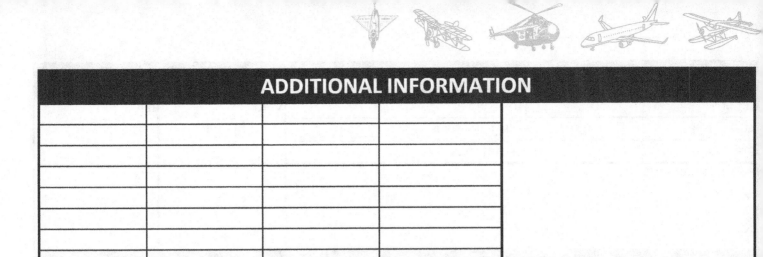

ADDITIONAL INFORMATION

SKECTH

NOTES

DATE: _____

FLIGHT INFORMATIONS

FROM		TO		VFR	IFR
ACRFT. TYPE		ACRFT. ID / FLT #	_____ I _____	☐	☐
ETE (Est. Flight Time)		DEPART. TIME (Zulu)			

ROUTE / WAYPOINTS	WIND	WX
>		
>	____ / ____	
>		

DEPARTURE

GATE / RUNWAY		PAYLOAD		ATC INSTRUCTIONS	
ALTIMETER		RESERVE		>	
CLIMB RATE		QNH		>	
TRANS ALT		SID		>	
ZFW		SQUAWK		>	
TOW		ATIS INFO		>	
BLOCK FUEL		>		>	
TAXIWAYS > RNW				>	

TAKE OFF / CLIMB / CRUISE PHASE

V_1:	V_R:	V_2:

EST. TOP OF CLIMB	ATC ACTUAL TOP OF CLIMB
>	>
EST. CRUISE FLIGHT LEVEL	ATC ACTUAL CRUISE FLIGHT LEVEL
>	>

DESCENT PHASE / APPROACH

TOP OF DESCENT	TRANSITION ALTITUDE	
>	>	

STAR		FIELD ELEVATION		Remarks
QNH		MAG / WIND		>
ATIS INFO				

GO AROUND (ALT / HDG / WAYPOINT)	>	

RNW / GATE		V_{APP} (Approach Speed) :	V_{REF} (Landing Speed) :
TAXIWAYS > GATE		>	>

DEPARTURE		∨	COMMS	ARRIVAL		∨
			REMARKS / NOTES			
GROUND				GROUND		
TOWER				TOWER		
CLEARANCE				APPROACH		
CONTROL				CONTROL		
RADAR				ILS		
ATIS / INFO				ATIS / INFO		
VATSIM				VATSIM		
IVAO				IVAO		

ADDITIONAL INFORMATION

SKECTH

NOTES

DATE: _____

FLIGHT INFORMATIONS

FROM		TO		**VFR**		**IFR**	
ACRFT. TYPE		ACRFT. ID / FLT #	_____ I _____	☐		☐	
ETE (Est. Flight Time)		DEPART. TIME (Zulu)					

ROUTE / WAYPOINTS	**WIND**	**WX**
> > >	_____ / ____	

DEPARTURE

GATE / RUNWAY		PAYLOAD		**ATC INSTRUCTIONS**
ALTIMETER		RESERVE		>
CLIMB RATE		QNH		>
TRANS ALT		SID		>
ZFW		SQUAWK		>
TOW		ATIS INFO		>
BLOCK FUEL		>		>
TAXIWAYS > RNW				>

TAKE OFF / CLIMB / CRUISE PHASE

V_1:	V_R:	V_2:

EST. TOP OF CLIMB	**ATC ACTUAL TOP OF CLIMB**
>	>

EST. CRUISE FLIGHT LEVEL	**ATC ACTUAL CRUISE FLIGHT LEVEL**
>	>

DESCENT PHASE / APPROACH

TOP OF DESCENT	TRANSITION ALTITUDE
>	>

STAR		FIELD ELEVATION		*Remarks*
QNH		MAG / WIND		>
ATIS INFO				

GO AROUND (ALT / HDG / WAYPOINT)	>	

RNW / GATE		V_{APP} (Approach Speed):	V_{REF} (Landing Speed):
TAXIWAYS > GATE		>	>

DEPARTURE ⊻		**COMMS**	**ARRIVAL** ⊻	
		REMARKS / NOTES		
GROUND			GROUND	
TOWER			TOWER	
CLEARANCE			APPROACH	
CONTROL			CONTROL	
RADAR			ILS	
ATIS / INFO			ATIS / INFO	
VATSIM			VATSIM	
IVAO			IVAO	

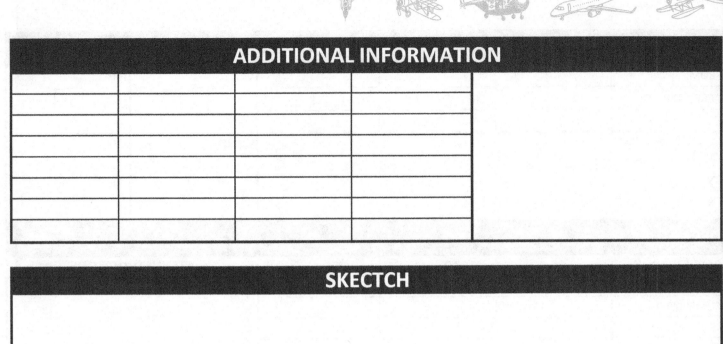

ADDITIONAL INFORMATION

SKECTCH

NOTES

DATE: _____

FLIGHT INFORMATIONS

FROM		TO		VFR		IFR	
ACRFT. TYPE		ACRFT. ID / FLT #	_____ I _____	☐		☐	
ETE (Est. Flight Time)		DEPART. TIME (Zulu)					

ROUTE / WAYPOINTS	WIND	WX
>	_____ / _____	
>		
>		

DEPARTURE

GATE / RUNWAY		PAYLOAD		ATC INSTRUCTIONS	
ALTIMETER		RESERVE		>	
CLIMB RATE		QNH		>	
TRANS ALT		SID		>	
ZFW		SQUAWK		>	
TOW		ATIS INFO		>	
BLOCK FUEL		>		>	
TAXIWAYS > RNW				>	

TAKE OFF / CLIMB / CRUISE PHASE

V_1:	V_R:	V_2:

EST. TOP OF CLIMB	ATC ACTUAL TOP OF CLIMB
>	>

EST. CRUISE FLIGHT LEVEL	ATC ACTUAL CRUISE FLIGHT LEVEL
>	>

DESCENT PHASE / APPROACH

TOP OF DESCENT	TRANSITION ALTITUDE
>	>

STAR		FIELD ELEVATION		Remarks
QNH		MAG / WIND		>
ATIS INFO				

GO AROUND (ALT / HDG / WAYPOINT)	>	

RNW / GATE		V_{APP} (Approach Speed):	V_{REF} (Landing Speed):
TAXIWAYS > GATE		>	>

DEPARTURE ⌄		COMMS	ARRIVAL ⌄	
		REMARKS / NOTES		
GROUND			GROUND	
TOWER			TOWER	
CLEARANCE			APPROACH	
CONTROL			CONTROL	
RADAR			ILS	
ATIS / INFO			ATIS / INFO	
VATSIM			VATSIM	
IVAO			IVAO	

ADDITIONAL INFORMATION

SKECTCH

NOTES

DATE: _____

FLIGHT INFORMATIONS

FROM		TO		VFR	IFR
ACRFT. TYPE		ACRFT. ID / FLT #	_____ I _____	☐	☐
ETE *(Est. Flight Time)*		DEPART. TIME *(Zulu)*			

ROUTE / WAYPOINTS	WIND	WX
> > >	_____ / _____	

DEPARTURE

GATE / RUNWAY		PAYLOAD		ATC INSTRUCTIONS
ALTIMETER		RESERVE		>
CLIMB RATE		QNH		>
TRANS ALT		SID		>
ZFW		SQUAWK		>
TOW		ATIS INFO		>
BLOCK FUEL		>		>
TAXIWAYS > RNW				>

TAKE OFF / CLIMB / CRUISE PHASE

V_1:	V_R:	V_2:

EST. TOP OF CLIMB	ATC ACTUAL TOP OF CLIMB
>	>

EST. CRUISE FLIGHT LEVEL	ATC ACTUAL CRUISE FLIGHT LEVEL
>	>

DESCENT PHASE / APPROACH

TOP OF DESCENT	TRANSITION ALTITUDE
>	>

STAR		FIELD ELEVATION		*Remarks*
QNH		MAG / WIND		>
ATIS INFO				

GO AROUND *(ALT / HDG / WAYPOINT)* >

RNW / GATE		V_{APP} *(Approach Speed)* :	V_{REF} *(Landing Speed)* :
TAXIWAYS > GATE		>	>

DEPARTURE ⌄	COMMS	*ARRIVAL* ⌄
	REMARKS / NOTES	

GROUND			GROUND	
TOWER			TOWER	
CLEARANCE			APPROACH	
CONTROL			CONTROL	
RADAR			ILS	
ATIS / INFO			ATIS / INFO	
VATSIM			VATSIM	
IVAO			IVAO	

ADDITIONAL INFORMATION

SKECTH

NOTES

DATE: _____

FLIGHT INFORMATIONS

FROM		TO		VFR	IFR
ACRFT. TYPE		ACRFT. ID / FLT #	_____ I _____	☐	☐
ETE (Est. Flight Time)		DEPART. TIME (Zulu)			

ROUTE / WAYPOINTS	WIND	WX
> > >	_____ / _____	

DEPARTURE

GATE / RUNWAY		PAYLOAD		ATC INSTRUCTIONS
ALTIMETER		RESERVE		>
CLIMB RATE		QNH		>
TRANS ALT		SID		>
ZFW		SQUAWK		>
TOW		ATIS INFO		>
BLOCK FUEL		>		>
TAXIWAYS > RNW				>

TAKE OFF / CLIMB / CRUISE PHASE

V_1:	V_R:	V_2:

EST. TOP OF CLIMB	ATC ACTUAL TOP OF CLIMB
>	>
EST. CRUISE FLIGHT LEVEL	ATC ACTUAL CRUISE FLIGHT LEVEL
>	>

DESCENT PHASE / APPROACH

TOP OF DESCENT	TRANSITION ALTITUDE
>	>

STAR		FIELD ELEVATION		Remarks
QNH		MAG / WIND		>
ATIS INFO				

GO AROUND (ALT / HDG / WAYPOINT)	>	

RNW / GATE		V_{APP} (Approach Speed):	V_{REF} (Landing Speed):
TAXIWAYS > GATE		>	>

DEPARTURE 📶 ˅	COMMS	ARRIVAL 📶 ˅
	REMARKS / NOTES	
GROUND		GROUND
TOWER		TOWER
CLEARANCE		APPROACH
CONTROL		CONTROL
RADAR		ILS
ATIS / INFO		ATIS / INFO
VATSIM		VATSIM
IVAO		IVAO

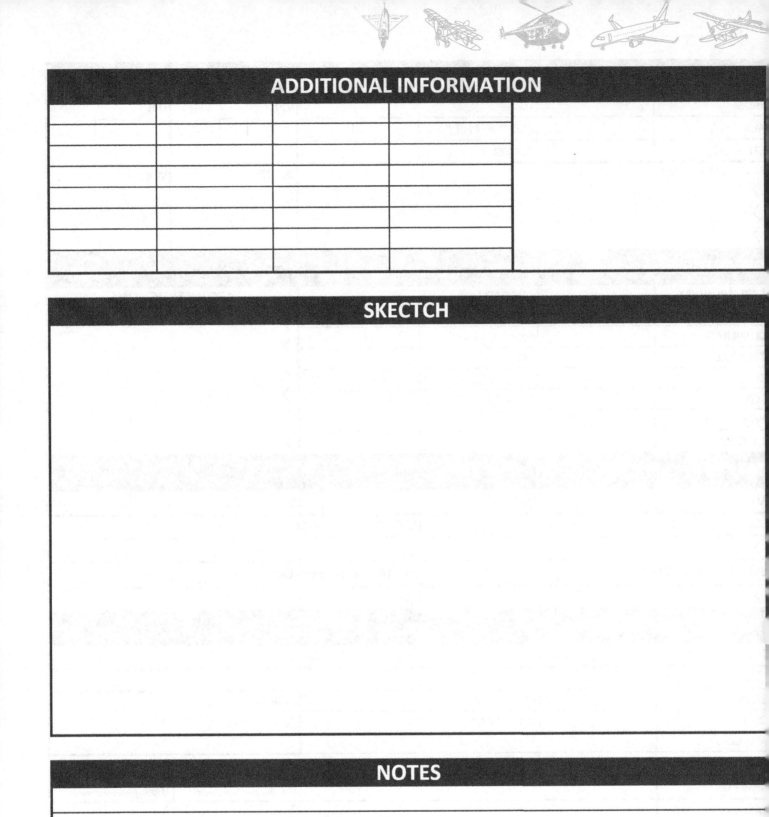

ADDITIONAL INFORMATION

SKECTCH

NOTES

DATE: _____

FLIGHT INFORMATIONS

FROM		TO		**VFR** ☐	**IFR** ☐
ACRFT. TYPE		ACRFT. ID / FLT #	_____ I _____		
ETE *(Est. Flight Time)*		DEPART. TIME *(Zulu)*			

ROUTE / WAYPOINTS	**WIND**	**WX**
>	____ / ____	
>		
>		

DEPARTURE

GATE / RUNWAY		PAYLOAD		**ATC INSTRUCTIONS**
ALTIMETER		RESERVE		>
CLIMB RATE		QNH		>
TRANS ALT		SID		>
ZFW		SQUAWK		>
TOW		ATIS INFO		>
BLOCK FUEL		>		>
TAXIWAYS > RNW				>

TAKE OFF / CLIMB / CRUISE PHASE

V_1:		V_R:		V_2:

EST. TOP OF CLIMB	ATC ACTUAL TOP OF CLIMB
>	>

EST. CRUISE FLIGHT LEVEL	ATC ACTUAL CRUISE FLIGHT LEVEL
>	>

DESCENT PHASE / APPROACH

TOP OF DESCENT	TRANSITION ALTITUDE
>	>

STAR		FIELD ELEVATION		*Remarks*
QNH		MAG / WIND		>
ATIS INFO				

GO AROUND *(ALT / HDG / WAYPOINT)*	>	

RNW / GATE		V_{APP} *(Approach Speed)* :	V_{REF} *(Landing Speed)* :
TAXIWAYS > GATE		>	>

DEPARTURE ⌄		COMMS	*ARRIVAL* ⌄	
GROUND		**REMARKS / NOTES**	GROUND	
TOWER			TOWER	
CLEARANCE			APPROACH	
CONTROL			CONTROL	
RADAR			ILS	
ATIS / INFO			ATIS / INFO	
VATSIM			VATSIM	
IVAO			IVAO	

ADDITIONAL INFORMATION

SKECTCH

NOTES

DATE: _____

FLIGHT INFORMATIONS

FROM		TO		VFR		IFR	
ACRFT. TYPE		ACRFT. ID / FLT #	____ I ____	☐		☐	
ETE *(Est. Flight Time)*		DEPART. TIME *(Zulu)*					

ROUTE / WAYPOINTS	WIND	WX
>	____ / ____	
>		
>		

DEPARTURE

				ATC INSTRUCTIONS	
GATE / RUNWAY		PAYLOAD			
ALTIMETER		RESERVE		>	
CLIMB RATE		QNH		>	
TRANS ALT		SID		>	
ZFW		SQUAWK		>	
TOW		ATIS INFO		>	
BLOCK FUEL		>		>	
TAXIWAYS > RNW				>	

TAKE OFF / CLIMB / CRUISE PHASE

V_1:	V_R:	V_2:

EST. TOP OF CLIMB	ATC ACTUAL TOP OF CLIMB
>	>

EST. CRUISE FLIGHT LEVEL	ATC ACTUAL CRUISE FLIGHT LEVEL
>	>

DESCENT PHASE / APPROACH

TOP OF DESCENT	TRANSITION ALTITUDE
>	>

STAR		FIELD ELEVATION		*Remarks*
QNH		MAG / WIND		>
ATIS INFO				

GO AROUND *(ALT / HDG / WAYPOINT)*	>	

RNW / GATE		V_{APP} *(Approach Speed)* :	V_{REF} *(Landing Speed)* :
TAXIWAYS > GATE		>	>

DEPARTURE ⌄		COMMS	*ARRIVAL* ⌄	
		REMARKS / NOTES		
GROUND			GROUND	
TOWER			TOWER	
CLEARANCE			APPROACH	
CONTROL			CONTROL	
RADAR			ILS	
ATIS / INFO			ATIS / INFO	
VATSIM			VATSIM	
IVAO			IVAO	

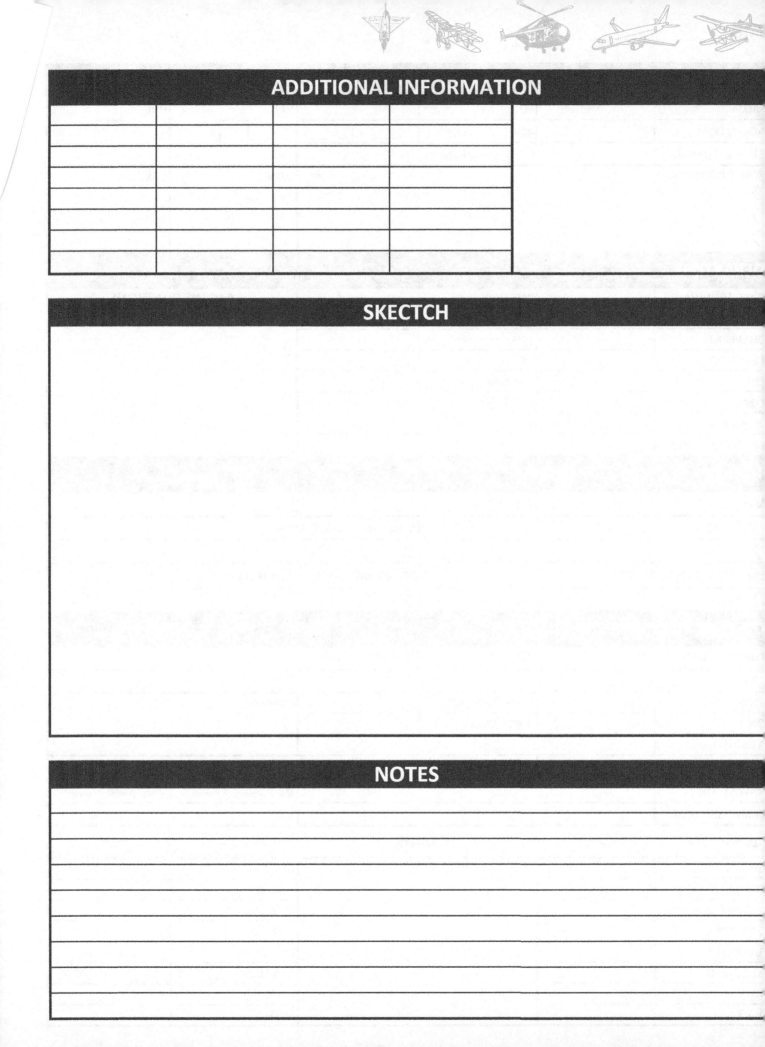

ADDITIONAL INFORMATION

SKECTCH

NOTES

DATE: _____

FLIGHT INFORMATIONS

FROM		TO		**VFR**		**IFR**	
ACRFT. TYPE		ACRFT. ID / FLT #	_____ I _____	☐		☐	
ETE *(Est. Flight Time)*		DEPART. TIME *(Zulu)*					

ROUTE / WAYPOINTS	**WIND**	**WX**
> > >	_____ / _____	

DEPARTURE

GATE / RUNWAY		PAYLOAD		**ATC INSTRUCTIONS**
ALTIMETER		RESERVE		>
CLIMB RATE		QNH		>
TRANS ALT		SID		>
ZFW		SQUAWK		>
TOW		ATIS INFO		>
BLOCK FUEL		>		>
TAXIWAYS > RNW				>

TAKE OFF / CLIMB / CRUISE PHASE

V_1:		V_R:		V_2:	

EST. TOP OF CLIMB	**ATC ACTUAL TOP OF CLIMB**
>	>
EST. CRUISE FLIGHT LEVEL	**ATC ACTUAL CRUISE FLIGHT LEVEL**
>	>

DESCENT PHASE / APPROACH

TOP OF DESCENT	TRANSITION ALTITUDE
>	>

STAR		FIELD ELEVATION		*Remarks*
QNH		MAG / WIND		>
ATIS INFO				

GO AROUND *(ALT / HDG / WAYPOINT)*	>	

RNW / GATE		V_{APP} *(Approach Speed)* :	V_{REF} *(Landing Speed)* :
TAXIWAYS > GATE		>	>

DEPARTURE ⌄		**COMMS**	*ARRIVAL* ⌄	
GROUND		**REMARKS / NOTES**	GROUND	
TOWER			TOWER	
CLEARANCE			APPROACH	
CONTROL			CONTROL	
RADAR			ILS	
ATIS / INFO			ATIS / INFO	
VATSIM			VATSIM	
IVAO			IVAO	

ADDITIONAL INFORMATION

SKECTCH

NOTES

DATE: _____

FLIGHT INFORMATIONS

FROM		TO		VFR ☐	IFR ☐
ACRFT. TYPE		ACRFT. ID / FLT #	_____ I _____		
ETE *(Est. Flight Time)*		DEPART. TIME *(Zulu)*			

ROUTE / WAYPOINTS	WIND ____ / ____	WX
>		
>		
>		

DEPARTURE

GATE / RUNWAY		PAYLOAD		**ATC INSTRUCTIONS**
ALTIMETER		RESERVE		>
CLIMB RATE		QNH		>
TRANS ALT		SID		>
ZFW		SQUAWK		>
TOW		ATIS INFO		>
BLOCK FUEL		>		>
TAXIWAYS > RNW				>

TAKE OFF / CLIMB / CRUISE PHASE

V_1:	V_R:	V_2:

EST. TOP OF CLIMB	ATC ACTUAL TOP OF CLIMB
>	>

EST. CRUISE FLIGHT LEVEL	ATC ACTUAL CRUISE FLIGHT LEVEL
>	>

DESCENT PHASE / APPROACH

TOP OF DESCENT	TRANSITION ALTITUDE
>	>

STAR		FIELD ELEVATION		*Remarks*
QNH		MAG / WIND		>
ATIS INFO				

GO AROUND *(ALT / HDG / WAYPOINT)*	>	

RNW / GATE		V_{APP} *(Approach Speed)* :	V_{REF} *(Landing Speed)* :
TAXIWAYS > GATE		>	>

DEPARTURE	⌄	**COMMS**	*ARRIVAL*	⌄
		REMARKS / NOTES		

DEPARTURE		ARRIVAL	
GROUND		GROUND	
TOWER		TOWER	
CLEARANCE		APPROACH	
CONTROL		CONTROL	
RADAR		ILS	
ATIS / INFO		ATIS / INFO	
VATSIM		VATSIM	
IVAO		IVAO	

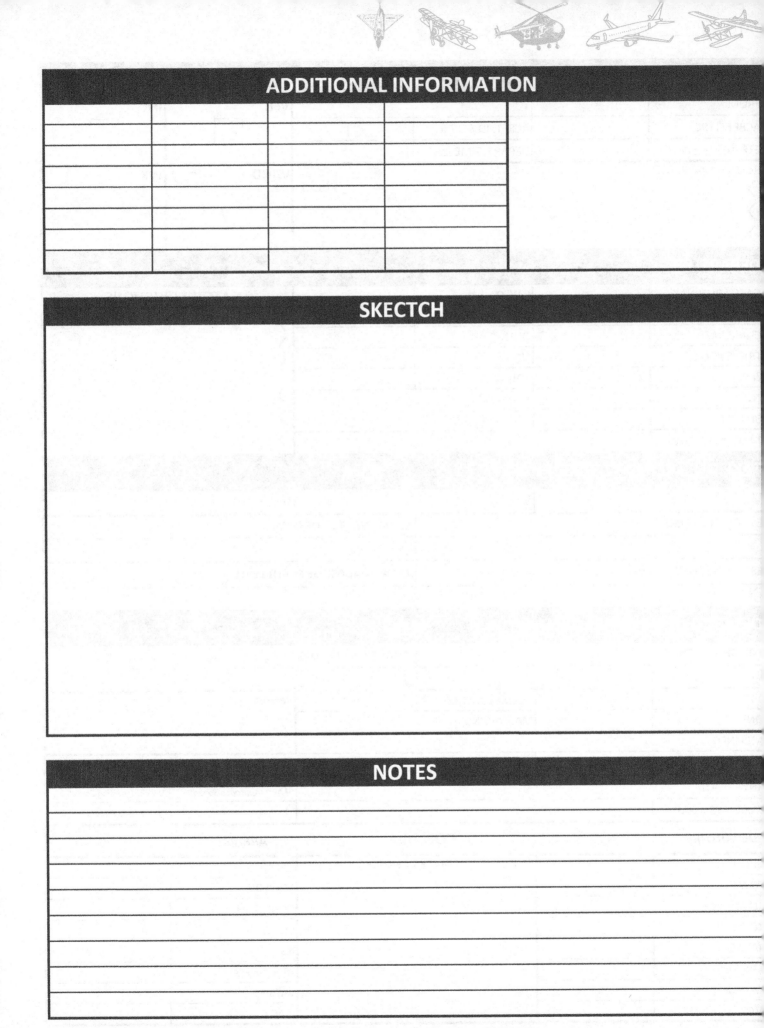

ADDITIONAL INFORMATION

SKECTCH

NOTES

DATE: _____

FLIGHT INFORMATIONS

FROM		TO		VFR ☐	IFR ☐
ACRFT. TYPE		ACRFT. ID / FLT #	_____ I _____		
ETE *(Est. Flight Time)*		DEPART. TIME *(Zulu)*			

ROUTE / WAYPOINTS	WIND	WX
>		
>	____ / ____	
>		

DEPARTURE

GATE / RUNWAY		PAYLOAD		ATC INSTRUCTIONS	
ALTIMETER		RESERVE		>	
CLIMB RATE		QNH		>	
TRANS ALT		SID		>	
ZFW		SQUAWK		>	
TOW		ATIS INFO		>	
BLOCK FUEL		>		>	
TAXIWAYS > RNW				>	

TAKE OFF / CLIMB / CRUISE PHASE

V_1:	V_R:	V_2:

EST. TOP OF CLIMB	ATC ACTUAL TOP OF CLIMB
>	>

EST. CRUISE FLIGHT LEVEL	ATC ACTUAL CRUISE FLIGHT LEVEL
>	>

DESCENT PHASE / APPROACH

TOP OF DESCENT	TRANSITION ALTITUDE
>	>

STAR		FIELD ELEVATION		Remarks
QNH		MAG / WIND		>
ATIS INFO				

GO AROUND *(ALT / HDG / WAYPOINT)*	>	

RNW / GATE		V_{APP} *(Approach Speed)* :	V_{REF} *(Landing Speed)* :
TAXIWAYS > GATE		>	>

DEPARTURE ⌄	COMMS	ARRIVAL ⌄
GROUND	REMARKS / NOTES	GROUND
TOWER		TOWER
CLEARANCE		APPROACH
CONTROL		CONTROL
RADAR		ILS
ATIS / INFO		ATIS / INFO
VATSIM		VATSIM
VAO		IVAO

ADDITIONAL INFORMATION

SKETCH

NOTES

DATE: _____

FLIGHT INFORMATIONS

FROM		TO		VFR	IFR
ACRFT. TYPE		ACRFT. ID / FLT #	_____ l _____	☐	☐
ETE *(Est. Flight Time)*		DEPART. TIME *(Zulu)*			

ROUTE / WAYPOINTS	WIND	WX
>	____ / ____	
>		
>		

DEPARTURE

GATE / RUNWAY		PAYLOAD		ATC INSTRUCTIONS	
ALTIMETER		RESERVE		>	
CLIMB RATE		QNH		>	
TRANS ALT		SID		>	
ZFW		SQUAWK		>	
TOW		ATIS INFO		>	
BLOCK FUEL		>		>	
TAXIWAYS > RNW				>	

TAKE OFF / CLIMB / CRUISE PHASE

V_1:		V_R:		V_2:

EST. TOP OF CLIMB	ATC ACTUAL TOP OF CLIMB
>	>
EST. CRUISE FLIGHT LEVEL	ATC ACTUAL CRUISE FLIGHT LEVEL
>	>

DESCENT PHASE / APPROACH

TOP OF DESCENT	TRANSITION ALTITUDE
>	>

STAR		FIELD ELEVATION		*Remarks*
QNH		MAG / WIND		>
ATIS INFO				

GO AROUND *(ALT / HDG / WAYPOINT)*	>	

RNW / GATE		V_{APP} *(Approach Speed)*:	V_{REF} *(Landing Speed)*:
TAXIWAYS > GATE		>	>

DEPARTURE		COMMS	ARRIVAL	
GROUND		REMARKS / NOTES	GROUND	
TOWER			TOWER	
CLEARANCE			APPROACH	
CONTROL			CONTROL	
RADAR			ILS	
ATIS / INFO			ATIS / INFO	
VATSIM			VATSIM	
IVAO			IVAO	

ADDITIONAL INFORMATION

SKECTCH

NOTES

DATE: _____

FLIGHT INFORMATIONS

FROM		TO		VFR	IFR
ACRFT. TYPE		ACRFT. ID / FLT #	_____ I _____	☐	☐
ETE *(Est. Flight Time)*		DEPART. TIME *(Zulu)*			

ROUTE / WAYPOINTS	WIND	WX
> > >	_____ / _____	

DEPARTURE

				ATC INSTRUCTIONS
GATE / RUNWAY		PAYLOAD		>
ALTIMETER		RESERVE		>
CLIMB RATE		QNH		>
TRANS ALT		SID		>
ZFW		SQUAWK		>
TOW		ATIS INFO		>
BLOCK FUEL		>		>
TAXIWAYS > RNW				>

TAKE OFF / CLIMB / CRUISE PHASE

V_1:	V_R:	V_2:

EST. TOP OF CLIMB	ATC ACTUAL TOP OF CLIMB
>	>

EST. CRUISE FLIGHT LEVEL	ATC ACTUAL CRUISE FLIGHT LEVEL
>	>

DESCENT PHASE / APPROACH

TOP OF DESCENT	TRANSITION ALTITUDE
>	>

STAR		FIELD ELEVATION		*Remarks*
QNH		MAG / WIND		>
ATIS INFO				

GO AROUND *(ALT / HDG / WAYPOINT)*	>	

RNW / GATE		V_{APP} *(Approach Speed)* :	V_{REF} *(Landing Speed)* :
TAXIWAYS > GATE		>	>

DEPARTURE ⌄	COMMS	*ARRIVAL* ⌄

		REMARKS / NOTES		
GROUND			GROUND	
TOWER			TOWER	
CLEARANCE			APPROACH	
CONTROL			CONTROL	
RADAR			ILS	
ATIS / INFO			ATIS / INFO	
VATSIM			VATSIM	
IVAO			IVAO	

ADDITIONAL INFORMATION

SKECTCH

NOTES

DATE: _____

FLIGHT INFORMATIONS

FROM		TO		VFR		IFR	
ACRFT. TYPE		ACRFT. ID / FLT #	_____ I _____	☐		☐	
ETE *(Est. Flight Time)*		DEPART. TIME *(Zulu)*					

ROUTE / WAYPOINTS	WIND	WX
>		
>	____ / ___	
>		

DEPARTURE

GATE / RUNWAY		PAYLOAD		ATC INSTRUCTIONS	
ALTIMETER		RESERVE		>	
CLIMB RATE		QNH		>	
TRANS ALT		SID		>	
ZFW		SQUAWK		>	
TOW		ATIS INFO		>	
BLOCK FUEL		>		>	
TAXIWAYS > RNW				>	

TAKE OFF / CLIMB / CRUISE PHASE

V_1:		V_R:		V_2:	

EST. TOP OF CLIMB	ATC ACTUAL TOP OF CLIMB
>	>

EST. CRUISE FLIGHT LEVEL	ATC ACTUAL CRUISE FLIGHT LEVEL
>	>

DESCENT PHASE / APPROACH

TOP OF DESCENT	TRANSITION ALTITUDE
>	>

STAR		FIELD ELEVATION		Remarks
QNH		MAG / WIND		>
ATIS INFO				

GO AROUND *(ALT / HDG / WAYPOINT)*	>	

RNW / GATE		V_{APP} *(Approach Speed)* :	V_{REF} *(Landing Speed)* :
TAXIWAYS > GATE		>	>

DEPARTURE		∨	COMMS	ARRIVAL		∨
GROUND			REMARKS / NOTES	GROUND		
TOWER				TOWER		
CLEARANCE				APPROACH		
CONTROL				CONTROL		
RADAR				ILS		
ATIS / INFO				ATIS / INFO		
VATSIM				VATSIM		
IVAO				IVAO		

ADDITIONAL INFORMATION

SKECTCH

NOTES

DATE: _____

FLIGHT INFORMATIONS

FROM		TO		**VFR**		**IFR**	
ACRFT. TYPE		ACRFT. ID / FLT #	_____ I _____	☐		☐	
ETE *(Est. Flight Time)*		DEPART. TIME *(Zulu)*					

ROUTE / WAYPOINTS	**WIND**	**WX**
>		
>	_____ / _____	
>		

DEPARTURE

GATE / RUNWAY		PAYLOAD		ATC INSTRUCTIONS	
ALTIMETER		RESERVE		>	
CLIMB RATE		QNH		>	
TRANS ALT		SID		>	
ZFW		SQUAWK		>	
TOW		ATIS INFO		>	
BLOCK FUEL		>		>	
TAXIWAYS > RNW				>	

TAKE OFF / CLIMB / CRUISE PHASE

V_1:		V_R:		V_2:	

EST. TOP OF CLIMB	ATC ACTUAL TOP OF CLIMB
>	>

EST. CRUISE FLIGHT LEVEL	ATC ACTUAL CRUISE FLIGHT LEVEL
>	>

DESCENT PHASE / APPROACH

TOP OF DESCENT	TRANSITION ALTITUDE
>	>

STAR		FIELD ELEVATION		*Remarks*
QNH		MAG / WIND		>
ATIS INFO				

GO AROUND *(ALT / HDG / WAYPOINT)*	>	

RNW / GATE		V_{APP} *(Approach Speed)* :	V_{REF} *(Landing Speed)* :
TAXIWAYS > GATE		>	>

DEPARTURE			**COMMS**	*ARRIVAL*		
GROUND			**REMARKS / NOTES**	GROUND	
TOWER				TOWER	
CLEARANCE				APPROACH	
CONTROL				CONTROL	
RADAR				ILS	
ATIS / INFO				ATIS / INFO	
VATSIM				VATSIM	
IVAO				IVAO	

ADDITIONAL INFORMATION

SKECTCH

NOTES

DATE: _____

FLIGHT INFORMATIONS

FROM		TO		VFR	IFR
ACRFT. TYPE		ACRFT. ID / FLT #	_____ I _____	☐	☐
ETE *(Est. Flight Time)*		DEPART. TIME *(Zulu)*			

ROUTE / WAYPOINTS	WIND	WX
>	_____ / ___	
>		
>		

DEPARTURE

GATE / RUNWAY		PAYLOAD		ATC INSTRUCTIONS
ALTIMETER		RESERVE		>
CLIMB RATE		QNH		>
TRANS ALT		SID		>
ZFW		SQUAWK		>
TOW		ATIS INFO		>
BLOCK FUEL		>		>
TAXIWAYS > RNW				>

TAKE OFF / CLIMB / CRUISE PHASE

V_1:		V_R:		V_2:

EST. TOP OF CLIMB	ATC ACTUAL TOP OF CLIMB
>	>

EST. CRUISE FLIGHT LEVEL	ATC ACTUAL CRUISE FLIGHT LEVEL
>	>

DESCENT PHASE / APPROACH

TOP OF DESCENT	TRANSITION ALTITUDE
>	>

STAR		FIELD ELEVATION		*Remarks*
QNH		MAG / WIND		>
ATIS INFO				

GO AROUND *(ALT / HDG / WAYPOINT)*	>	

RNW / GATE		V_{APP} *(Approach Speed)* :	V_{REF} *(Landing Speed)* :
TAXIWAYS > GATE		>	>

DEPARTURE			COMMS	*ARRIVAL*		
GROUND		REMARKS / NOTES		GROUND	
TOWER				TOWER	
CLEARANCE				APPROACH	
CONTROL				CONTROL	
RADAR				ILS	
ATIS / INFO				ATIS / INFO	
VATSIM				VATSIM	
IVAO				IVAO	

ADDITIONAL INFORMATION

SKECTCH

NOTES

DATE: _____

FLIGHT INFORMATIONS

FROM		TO		VFR		IFR	
ACRFT. TYPE		ACRFT. ID / FLT #	_____ I _____	☐		☐	
ETE *(Est. Flight Time)*		DEPART. TIME *(Zulu)*					

ROUTE / WAYPOINTS	WIND	WX
> > >	____ / ___	

DEPARTURE

GATE / RUNWAY		PAYLOAD		ATC INSTRUCTIONS	
ALTIMETER		RESERVE		>	
CLIMB RATE		QNH		>	
TRANS ALT		SID		>	
ZFW		SQUAWK		>	
TOW		ATIS INFO		>	
BLOCK FUEL		>		>	
TAXIWAYS > RNW				>	

TAKE OFF / CLIMB / CRUISE PHASE

V_1:		V_R:		V_2:	

EST. TOP OF CLIMB	ATC ACTUAL TOP OF CLIMB
>	>

EST. CRUISE FLIGHT LEVEL	ATC ACTUAL CRUISE FLIGHT LEVEL
>	>

DESCENT PHASE / APPROACH

TOP OF DESCENT	TRANSITION ALTITUDE
>	>

STAR		FIELD ELEVATION		*Remarks*
QNH		MAG / WIND		>
ATIS INFO				

GO AROUND *(ALT / HDG / WAYPOINT)*	>	

RNW / GATE		V_{APP} *(Approach Speed)* :	V_{REF} *(Landing Speed)* :
TAXIWAYS > GATE		>	>

DEPARTURE 〉✓	COMMS	ARRIVAL 〉✓

GROUND		REMARKS / NOTES	GROUND	
TOWER			TOWER	
CLEARANCE			APPROACH	
CONTROL			CONTROL	
RADAR			ILS	
ATIS / INFO			ATIS / INFO	
VATSIM			VATSIM	
IVAO			IVAO	

ADDITIONAL INFORMATION

SKECTCH

NOTES

DATE: _____

FLIGHT INFORMATIONS

FROM		TO		VFR		IFR	
ACRFT. TYPE		ACRFT. ID / FLT #	_____ I _____	☐		☐	
ETE *(Est. Flight Time)*		DEPART. TIME *(Zulu)*					

ROUTE / WAYPOINTS	WIND	WX
>	____ / ____	
>		
>		

DEPARTURE

GATE / RUNWAY		PAYLOAD		ATC INSTRUCTIONS	
ALTIMETER		RESERVE		>	
CLIMB RATE		QNH		>	
TRANS ALT		SID		>	
ZFW		SQUAWK		>	
TOW		ATIS INFO		>	
BLOCK FUEL		>		>	
TAXIWAYS > RNW				>	

TAKE OFF / CLIMB / CRUISE PHASE

V₁:	VR:	V₂:

EST. TOP OF CLIMB	ATC ACTUAL TOP OF CLIMB
>	>

EST. CRUISE FLIGHT LEVEL	ATC ACTUAL CRUISE FLIGHT LEVEL
>	>

DESCENT PHASE / APPROACH

TOP OF DESCENT	TRANSITION ALTITUDE
>	>

STAR		FIELD ELEVATION		*Remarks*
QNH		MAG / WIND		>
ATIS INFO				

GO AROUND *(ALT / HDG / WAYPOINT)*	>	

RNW / GATE		VAPP *(Approach Speed)*:	VREF *(Landing Speed)*:
TAXIWAYS > GATE		>	>

DEPARTURE		COMMS	ARRIVAL	
		REMARKS / NOTES		
GROUND			GROUND	
TOWER			TOWER	
CLEARANCE			APPROACH	
CONTROL			CONTROL	
RADAR			ILS	
ATIS / INFO			ATIS / INFO	
VATSIM			VATSIM	
IVAO			IVAO	

ADDITIONAL INFORMATION

SKETCH

NOTES

DATE: _____

FLIGHT INFORMATIONS

FROM		TO		**VFR**		**IFR**	
ACRFT. TYPE		ACRFT. ID / FLT #	_____ I _____	☐		☐	
ETE *(Est. Flight Time)*		DEPART. TIME *(Zulu)*					

ROUTE / WAYPOINTS	**WIND**	**WX**
> > >	_____ / ____	

DEPARTURE

GATE / RUNWAY		PAYLOAD		**ATC INSTRUCTIONS**
ALTIMETER		RESERVE		>
CLIMB RATE		QNH		>
TRANS ALT		SID		>
ZFW		SQUAWK		>
TOW		ATIS INFO		>
BLOCK FUEL		>		>
TAXIWAYS > RNW				>

TAKE OFF / CLIMB / CRUISE PHASE

V_1:	V_R:	V_2:

EST. TOP OF CLIMB	**ATC ACTUAL TOP OF CLIMB**
>	>
EST. CRUISE FLIGHT LEVEL	**ATC ACTUAL CRUISE FLIGHT LEVEL**
>	>

DESCENT PHASE / APPROACH

TOP OF DESCENT	TRANSITION ALTITUDE
>	>

STAR		FIELD ELEVATION		*Remarks*
QNH		MAG / WIND		>
ATIS INFO				

GO AROUND *(ALT / HDG / WAYPOINT)*	>	

RNW / GATE		V_{APP} *(Approach Speed)* :	V_{REF} *(Landing Speed)* :
TAXIWAYS > GATE		>	>

DEPARTURE ⌄	**COMMS**	*ARRIVAL* ⌄
	REMARKS / NOTES	

DEPARTURE			ARRIVAL	
GROUND			GROUND	
TOWER			TOWER	
CLEARANCE			APPROACH	
CONTROL			CONTROL	
RADAR			ILS	
ATIS / INFO			ATIS / INFO	
VATSIM			VATSIM	
IVAO			IVAO	

ADDITIONAL INFORMATION

SKECTCH

NOTES

DATE: _____

FLIGHT INFORMATIONS

FROM		TO		VFR ☐	IFR ☐
ACRFT. TYPE		ACRFT. ID / FLT #	_____ I _____		
ETE *(Est. Flight Time)*		DEPART. TIME *(Zulu)*			

ROUTE / WAYPOINTS	WIND ____ / ____	WX
>		
>		
>		

DEPARTURE

GATE / RUNWAY		PAYLOAD		**ATC INSTRUCTIONS**
ALTIMETER		RESERVE		>
CLIMB RATE		QNH		>
TRANS ALT		SID		>
ZFW		SQUAWK		>
TOW		ATIS INFO		>
BLOCK FUEL		>		>
TAXIWAYS > RNW				>

TAKE OFF / CLIMB / CRUISE PHASE

| V_1: | V_R: | V_2: |

| EST. TOP OF CLIMB | ATC ACTUAL TOP OF CLIMB |
| > | > |

| EST. CRUISE FLIGHT LEVEL | ATC ACTUAL CRUISE FLIGHT LEVEL |
| > | > |

DESCENT PHASE / APPROACH

| TOP OF DESCENT | TRANSITION ALTITUDE |
| > | > |

STAR		FIELD ELEVATION		*Remarks*
QNH		MAG / WIND		>
ATIS INFO				

| GO AROUND *(ALT / HDG / WAYPOINT)* | > | |

| RNW / GATE | | V_{APP} *(Approach Speed)* : | V_{REF} *(Landing Speed)* : |
| TAXIWAYS > GATE | | > | > |

DEPARTURE ⌄	COMMS	ARRIVAL ⌄
GROUND		**REMARKS / NOTES**	GROUND	
TOWER			TOWER	
CLEARANCE			APPROACH	
CONTROL			CONTROL	
RADAR			ILS	
ATIS / INFO			ATIS / INFO	
VATSIM			VATSIM	
IVAO			IVAO	

ADDITIONAL INFORMATION

SKECTCH

NOTES

DATE: _____

FLIGHT INFORMATIONS

FROM		TO		VFR	IFR
ACRFT. TYPE		ACRFT. ID / FLT #	_____ I _____	☐	☐
ETE *(Est. Flight Time)*		DEPART. TIME *(Zulu)*			

ROUTE / WAYPOINTS 🗺️📍	WIND 🌬️ ____ / ____	WX ☀️⛅☁️🌧️⛈️
>		
>		
>		

DEPARTURE

GATE / RUNWAY		PAYLOAD		ATC INSTRUCTIONS 🎧
ALTIMETER		RESERVE		>
CLIMB RATE		QNH		>
TRANS ALT		SID		>
ZFW		SQUAWK		>
TOW		ATIS INFO		>
BLOCK FUEL		>		>
TAXIWAYS > RNW				>

TAKE OFF / CLIMB / CRUISE PHASE

V_1:	V_R:	V_2:

EST. TOP OF CLIMB	ATC ACTUAL TOP OF CLIMB
>	>

EST. CRUISE FLIGHT LEVEL	ATC ACTUAL CRUISE FLIGHT LEVEL
>	>

DESCENT PHASE / APPROACH

TOP OF DESCENT	TRANSITION ALTITUDE
>	>

STAR		FIELD ELEVATION		Remarks
QNH		MAG / WIND		>
ATIS INFO				

GO AROUND *(ALT / HDG / WAYPOINT)* >	

RNW / GATE		V_{APP} *(Approach Speed)*:	V_{REF} *(Landing Speed)*:
TAXIWAYS > GATE		>	>

DEPARTURE 📡 ⌄	COMMS	ARRIVAL 📡 ⌄

DEPARTURE		REMARKS / NOTES	ARRIVAL	
GROUND			GROUND	
TOWER			TOWER	
CLEARANCE			APPROACH	
CONTROL			CONTROL	
RADAR			ILS	
ATIS / INFO			ATIS / INFO	
VATSIM			VATSIM	
IVAO			IVAO	

ADDITIONAL INFORMATION

SKECTCH

NOTES

DATE: _____

FLIGHT INFORMATIONS

FROM		TO		VFR		IFR	
ACRFT. TYPE		ACRFT. ID / FLT #	_____ I _____	☐		☐	
ETE *(Est. Flight Time)*		DEPART. TIME *(Zulu)*					

ROUTE / WAYPOINTS	WIND	WX
>	_____ / ____	
>		
>		

DEPARTURE

GATE / RUNWAY		PAYLOAD		**ATC INSTRUCTIONS**	
ALTIMETER		RESERVE		>	
CLIMB RATE		QNH		>	
TRANS ALT		SID		>	
ZFW		SQUAWK		>	
TOW		ATIS INFO		>	
BLOCK FUEL		>		>	
TAXIWAYS > RNW				>	

TAKE OFF / CLIMB / CRUISE PHASE

V_1:	V_R:	V_2:

EST. TOP OF CLIMB	ATC ACTUAL TOP OF CLIMB
>	>
EST. CRUISE FLIGHT LEVEL	ATC ACTUAL CRUISE FLIGHT LEVEL
>	>

DESCENT PHASE / APPROACH

TOP OF DESCENT	TRANSITION ALTITUDE
>	>

STAR		FIELD ELEVATION		*Remarks*
QNH		MAG / WIND		>
ATIS INFO				

GO AROUND *(ALT / HDG / WAYPOINT)*	>	

RNW / GATE		V_{APP} *(Approach Speed)* :	V_{REF} *(Landing Speed)* :
TAXIWAYS > GATE		>	>

DEPARTURE		∨	COMMS	ARRIVAL		∨
GROUND			REMARKS / NOTES	GROUND		
TOWER				TOWER		
CLEARANCE				APPROACH		
CONTROL				CONTROL		
RADAR				ILS		
ATIS / INFO				ATIS / INFO		
VATSIM				VATSIM		
IVAO				IVAO		

ADDITIONAL INFORMATION

SKECTCH

NOTES

DATE: _____

FLIGHT INFORMATIONS

FROM		TO		**VFR** ☐	**IFR** ☐
ACRFT. TYPE		ACRFT. ID / FLT #	_____ I _____		
ETE *(Est. Flight Time)*		DEPART. TIME *(Zulu)*			

ROUTE / WAYPOINTS	**WIND** _____ / _____	**WX**
>		
>		
>		

DEPARTURE

GATE / RUNWAY		PAYLOAD		**ATC INSTRUCTIONS**
ALTIMETER		RESERVE		>
CLIMB RATE		QNH		>
TRANS ALT		SID		>
ZFW		SQUAWK		>
TOW		ATIS INFO		>
BLOCK FUEL		>		>
TAXIWAYS > RNW				>

TAKE OFF / CLIMB / CRUISE PHASE

V_1:	V_R:	V_2:

EST. TOP OF CLIMB	ATC ACTUAL TOP OF CLIMB
>	>

EST. CRUISE FLIGHT LEVEL	ATC ACTUAL CRUISE FLIGHT LEVEL
>	>

DESCENT PHASE / APPROACH

TOP OF DESCENT	TRANSITION ALTITUDE
>	>

STAR		FIELD ELEVATION		*Remarks*
QNH		MAG / WIND		>
ATIS INFO				

GO AROUND *(ALT / HDG / WAYPOINT)*	>	

RNW / GATE		V_{APP} *(Approach Speed)* :	V_{REF} *(Landing Speed)* :
TAXIWAYS > GATE		>	>

DEPARTURE ⌄	COMMS	*ARRIVAL* ⌄

		REMARKS / NOTES		
GROUND			GROUND	
TOWER			TOWER	
CLEARANCE			APPROACH	
CONTROL			CONTROL	
RADAR			ILS	
ATIS / INFO			ATIS / INFO	
VATSIM			VATSIM	
IVAO			IVAO	

DATE: _____

FLIGHT INFORMATIONS

FROM		TO		VFR		IFR	
ACRFT. TYPE		ACRFT. ID / FLT #	_____ I _____	☐		☐	
ETE *(Est. Flight Time)*		DEPART. TIME *(Zulu)*					

ROUTE / WAYPOINTS 🗺️	WIND 🌬️	WX
> > >	____ / ____	☀️⛅☁️🌧️⛈️

DEPARTURE

GATE / RUNWAY		PAYLOAD		ATC INSTRUCTIONS
ALTIMETER		RESERVE		>
CLIMB RATE		QNH		>
TRANS ALT		SID		>
ZFW		SQUAWK		>
TOW		ATIS INFO		>
BLOCK FUEL		>		>
TAXIWAYS > RNW				>

TAKE OFF / CLIMB / CRUISE PHASE

V_1:		V_R:		V_2:

EST. TOP OF CLIMB	ATC ACTUAL TOP OF CLIMB
>	>

EST. CRUISE FLIGHT LEVEL	ATC ACTUAL CRUISE FLIGHT LEVEL
>	>

DESCENT PHASE / APPROACH

TOP OF DESCENT	TRANSITION ALTITUDE
>	>

STAR		FIELD ELEVATION		*Remarks*
QNH		MAG / WIND		>
ATIS INFO				

GO AROUND *(ALT / HDG / WAYPOINT)* >		

RNW / GATE		V_{APP} *(Approach Speed)* :	V_{REF} *(Landing Speed)* :
TAXIWAYS > GATE		>	>

DEPARTURE 📡 ⌄	COMMS	*ARRIVAL* 📡 ⌄
GROUND	**REMARKS / NOTES**	GROUND
TOWER		TOWER
CLEARANCE		APPROACH
CONTROL		CONTROL
RADAR		ILS
ATIS / INFO		ATIS / INFO
VATSIM		VATSIM
IVAO		IVAO

ADDITIONAL INFORMATION

SKECTCH

NOTES

DATE: _____

FLIGHT INFORMATIONS

FROM		TO		**VFR**		**IFR**	
ACRFT. TYPE		ACRFT. ID / FLT #	_____ I _____	☐		☐	
ETE (Est. Flight Time)		DEPART. TIME (Zulu)					

ROUTE / WAYPOINTS	🗺️	**WIND** 🌬️	**WX**
>			☀️ 🌤️ ☁️ 🌧️ ⛈️
>		____ / ____	
>			

DEPARTURE

GATE / RUNWAY		PAYLOAD		**ATC INSTRUCTIONS**	
ALTIMETER		RESERVE		>	🎧
CLIMB RATE		QNH		>	
TRANS ALT		SID		>	
ZFW		SQUAWK		>	
TOW		ATIS INFO		>	
BLOCK FUEL		>		>	
TAXIWAYS > RNW				>	

TAKE OFF / CLIMB / CRUISE PHASE

V_1:		V_R:		V_2:	

EST. TOP OF CLIMB	**ATC ACTUAL TOP OF CLIMB**
>	>

EST. CRUISE FLIGHT LEVEL	**ATC ACTUAL CRUISE FLIGHT LEVEL**
>	>

DESCENT PHASE / APPROACH

TOP OF DESCENT	TRANSITION ALTITUDE
>	>

STAR		FIELD ELEVATION		*Remarks*
QNH		MAG / WIND		>
ATIS INFO				

GO AROUND (ALT / HDG / WAYPOINT) >

RNW / GATE			V_{APP} (Approach Speed) :	V_{REF} (Landing Speed) :
TAXIWAYS > GATE			>	>

DEPARTURE 📡 ⌄		**COMMS**	*ARRIVAL* 📡 ⌄	
GROUND		**REMARKS / NOTES**	GROUND	
TOWER			TOWER	
CLEARANCE			APPROACH	
CONTROL			CONTROL	
RADAR			ILS	
ATIS / INFO			ATIS / INFO	
VATSIM			VATSIM	
IVAO			IVAO	

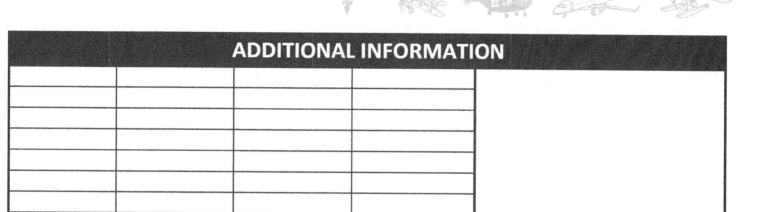

ADDITIONAL INFORMATION

SKETCH

NOTES

DATE: _____

FLIGHT INFORMATIONS

FROM		TO		VFR ☐	IFR ☐
ACRFT. TYPE		ACRFT. ID / FLT #	_____ I _____		
ETE *(Est. Flight Time)*		DEPART. TIME *(Zulu)*			

ROUTE / WAYPOINTS	WIND ____ / ____	WX
>		
>		
>		

DEPARTURE

GATE / RUNWAY		PAYLOAD		**ATC INSTRUCTIONS**	
ALTIMETER		RESERVE		>	
CLIMB RATE		QNH		>	
TRANS ALT		SID		>	
ZFW		SQUAWK		>	
TOW		ATIS INFO		>	
BLOCK FUEL		>		>	
TAXIWAYS > RNW					

TAKE OFF / CLIMB / CRUISE PHASE

V_1:	V_R:	V_2:

EST. TOP OF CLIMB	**ATC ACTUAL TOP OF CLIMB**
>	>
EST. CRUISE FLIGHT LEVEL	**ATC ACTUAL CRUISE FLIGHT LEVEL**
>	>

DESCENT PHASE / APPROACH

TOP OF DESCENT	TRANSITION ALTITUDE
>	>

STAR		FIELD ELEVATION		*Remarks*
QNH		MAG / WIND		>
ATIS INFO				

GO AROUND *(ALT / HDG / WAYPOINT)*	>	

RNW / GATE		V_{APP} *(Approach Speed)* :	V_{REF} *(Landing Speed)* :
TAXIWAYS > GATE		>	>

DEPARTURE		*COMMS*	*ARRIVAL*	
GROUND		**REMARKS / NOTES**	GROUND	
TOWER			TOWER	
CLEARANCE			APPROACH	
CONTROL			CONTROL	
RADAR			ILS	
ATIS / INFO			ATIS / INFO	
VATSIM			VATSIM	
IVAO			IVAO	

ADDITIONAL INFORMATION

SKECTCH

NOTES

DATE: _____

FLIGHT INFORMATIONS

FROM		TO		**VFR** ☐	**IFR** ☐
ACRFT. TYPE		ACRFT. ID / FLT #	_____ I _____		
ETE *(Est. Flight Time)*		DEPART. TIME *(Zulu)*			

ROUTE / WAYPOINTS		**WIND**	**WX**
>			
>		____ / ____	☀ ⛅ ☁ 🌧 ⛈
>			

DEPARTURE

GATE / RUNWAY		PAYLOAD		**ATC INSTRUCTIONS**
ALTIMETER		RESERVE		>
CLIMB RATE		QNH		>
TRANS ALT		SID		>
ZFW		SQUAWK		>
TOW		ATIS INFO		>
BLOCK FUEL		>		>
TAXIWAYS > RNW				>

TAKE OFF / CLIMB / CRUISE PHASE

V_1:	V_R:	V_2:

EST. TOP OF CLIMB	**ATC ACTUAL TOP OF CLIMB**
>	>
EST. CRUISE FLIGHT LEVEL	**ATC ACTUAL CRUISE FLIGHT LEVEL**
>	>

DESCENT PHASE / APPROACH

TOP OF DESCENT	TRANSITION ALTITUDE
>	>

STAR		FIELD ELEVATION		*Remarks*
QNH		MAG / WIND		>
ATIS INFO				

GO AROUND *(ALT / HDG / WAYPOINT)*	>	

RNW / GATE		V_{APP} *(Approach Speed)* :	V_{REF} *(Landing Speed)* :
TAXIWAYS > GATE		>	>

DEPARTURE 📶 ⌄	**COMMS**	*ARRIVAL* 📶 ⌄
GROUND	**REMARKS / NOTES**	GROUND
TOWER		TOWER
CLEARANCE		APPROACH
CONTROL		CONTROL
RADAR		ILS
ATIS / INFO		ATIS / INFO
VATSIM		VATSIM
IVAO		IVAO

ADDITIONAL INFORMATION

SKECTCH

NOTES

DATE: _____

FLIGHT INFORMATIONS

FROM		TO		VFR	☐	IFR	☐
ACRFT. TYPE		ACRFT. ID / FLT #	_____ I _____				
ETE *(Est. Flight Time)*		DEPART. TIME *(Zulu)*					

ROUTE / WAYPOINTS	WIND	WX
> > >	____ / ___	

DEPARTURE

GATE / RUNWAY		PAYLOAD		ATC INSTRUCTIONS	
ALTIMETER		RESERVE		>	
CLIMB RATE		QNH		>	
TRANS ALT		SID		>	
ZFW		SQUAWK		>	
TOW		ATIS INFO		>	
BLOCK FUEL		>		>	
TAXIWAYS > RNW				>	

TAKE OFF / CLIMB / CRUISE PHASE

V_1:	V_R:	V_2:

EST. TOP OF CLIMB	ATC ACTUAL TOP OF CLIMB
>	>

EST. CRUISE FLIGHT LEVEL	ATC ACTUAL CRUISE FLIGHT LEVEL
>	>

DESCENT PHASE / APPROACH

TOP OF DESCENT	TRANSITION ALTITUDE
>	>

STAR		FIELD ELEVATION		*Remarks*
QNH		MAG / WIND		>
ATIS INFO				

GO AROUND *(ALT / HDG / WAYPOINT)*	>	

RNW / GATE		V_{APP} *(Approach Speed)* :	V_{REF} *(Landing Speed)* :
TAXIWAYS > GATE		>	>

DEPARTURE		COMMS	*ARRIVAL*	
GROUND		REMARKS / NOTES	GROUND	
TOWER			TOWER	
CLEARANCE			APPROACH	
CONTROL			CONTROL	
RADAR			ILS	
ATIS / INFO			ATIS / INFO	
VATSIM			VATSIM	
IVAO			IVAO	

ADDITIONAL INFORMATION

SKECTCH

NOTES

DATE: _____

FLIGHT INFORMATIONS

FROM		TO		VFR ☐	IFR ☐
ACRFT. TYPE		ACRFT. ID / FLT #	_____ I _____		
ETE *(Est. Flight Time)*		DEPART. TIME *(Zulu)*			

ROUTE / WAYPOINTS	WIND	WX
>	____ / ____	
>		
>		

DEPARTURE

				ATC INSTRUCTIONS
GATE / RUNWAY		PAYLOAD		
ALTIMETER		RESERVE		>
CLIMB RATE		QNH		>
TRANS ALT		SID		>
ZFW		SQUAWK		>
TOW		ATIS INFO		>
BLOCK FUEL		>		>
TAXIWAYS > RNW				>

TAKE OFF / CLIMB / CRUISE PHASE

V₁:	VR:	V₂:

EST. TOP OF CLIMB	ATC ACTUAL TOP OF CLIMB
>	>

EST. CRUISE FLIGHT LEVEL	ATC ACTUAL CRUISE FLIGHT LEVEL
>	>

DESCENT PHASE / APPROACH

TOP OF DESCENT	TRANSITION ALTITUDE
>	>

STAR		FIELD ELEVATION		*Remarks*
QNH		MAG / WIND		>
ATIS INFO				

GO AROUND *(ALT / HDG / WAYPOINT)*	>		

RNW / GATE		V APP *(Approach Speed)* :	V REF *(Landing Speed)* :
TAXIWAYS > GATE		>	>

DEPARTURE		COMMS	ARRIVAL	
GROUND		**REMARKS / NOTES**	GROUND	
TOWER			TOWER	
CLEARANCE			APPROACH	
CONTROL			CONTROL	
RADAR			ILS	
ATIS / INFO			ATIS / INFO	
VATSIM			VATSIM	
IVAO			IVAO	

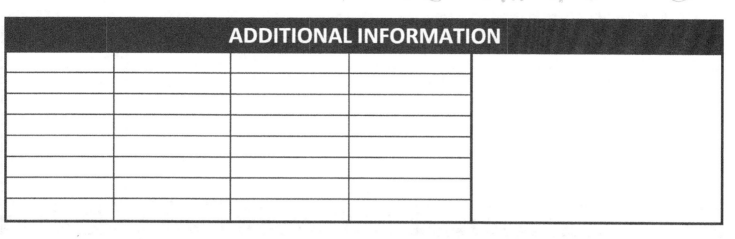

ADDITIONAL INFORMATION

SKECTH

NOTES

DATE: _____

FLIGHT INFORMATIONS

FROM		TO		**VFR**	☐	**IFR**	☐
ACRFT. TYPE		ACRFT. ID / FLT #	_____ I _____				
ETE *(Est. Flight Time)*		DEPART. TIME *(Zulu)*					

ROUTE / WAYPOINTS	**WIND**	**WX**
>		
>	_____ / _____	
>		

DEPARTURE

				ATC INSTRUCTIONS	
GATE / RUNWAY		PAYLOAD			
ALTIMETER		RESERVE		>	
CLIMB RATE		QNH		>	
TRANS ALT		SID		>	
ZFW		SQUAWK		>	
TOW		ATIS INFO		>	
BLOCK FUEL		>		>	
TAXIWAYS > RNW				>	

TAKE OFF / CLIMB / CRUISE PHASE

V_1:	V_R:	V_2:

EST. TOP OF CLIMB	ATC ACTUAL TOP OF CLIMB
>	>
EST. CRUISE FLIGHT LEVEL	ATC ACTUAL CRUISE FLIGHT LEVEL
>	>

DESCENT PHASE / APPROACH

TOP OF DESCENT	TRANSITION ALTITUDE
>	>

STAR		FIELD ELEVATION		*Remarks*
QNH		MAG / WIND		>
ATIS INFO				

GO AROUND *(ALT / HDG / WAYPOINT)*	>	

RNW / GATE		V_{APP} *(Approach Speed)* :	V_{REF} *(Landing Speed)* :
TAXIWAYS > GATE		>	>

DEPARTURE ⌄	**COMMS**	*ARRIVAL* ⌄
GROUND	**REMARKS / NOTES**	GROUND
TOWER		TOWER
CLEARANCE		APPROACH
CONTROL		CONTROL
RADAR		ILS
ATIS / INFO		ATIS / INFO
VATSIM		VATSIM
IVAO		IVAO

ADDITIONAL INFORMATION

SKECTCH

NOTES

DATE: _____

FLIGHT INFORMATIONS

FROM		TO		VFR	☐	IFR	☐
ACRFT. TYPE		ACRFT. ID / FLT #	____ I ____				
ETE *(Est. Flight Time)*		DEPART. TIME *(Zulu)*					

ROUTE / WAYPOINTS	WIND ___ / ___	WX
>		
>		
>		

DEPARTURE

GATE / RUNWAY		PAYLOAD		ATC INSTRUCTIONS	
ALTIMETER		RESERVE		>	
CLIMB RATE		QNH		>	
TRANS ALT		SID		>	
ZFW		SQUAWK		>	
TOW		ATIS INFO		>	
BLOCK FUEL		>		>	
TAXIWAYS > RNW				>	

TAKE OFF / CLIMB / CRUISE PHASE

V_1:		V_R:		V_2:

EST. TOP OF CLIMB	ATC ACTUAL TOP OF CLIMB
>	>

EST. CRUISE FLIGHT LEVEL	ATC ACTUAL CRUISE FLIGHT LEVEL
>	>

DESCENT PHASE / APPROACH

TOP OF DESCENT	TRANSITION ALTITUDE
>	>

STAR		FIELD ELEVATION		Remarks
QNH		MAG / WIND		>
ATIS INFO				

GO AROUND *(ALT / HDG / WAYPOINT)* >

RNW / GATE		V_{APP} *(Approach Speed)* :	V_{REF} *(Landing Speed)* :
TAXIWAYS > GATE		>	>

DEPARTURE		COMMS	ARRIVAL	
GROUND		**REMARKS / NOTES**	GROUND	
TOWER			TOWER	
CLEARANCE			APPROACH	
CONTROL			CONTROL	
RADAR			ILS	
ATIS / INFO			ATIS / INFO	
VATSIM			VATSIM	
IVAO			IVAO	

ADDITIONAL INFORMATION

SKECTCH

NOTES

DATE: _____

FLIGHT INFORMATIONS

FROM		TO		VFR ☐	IFR ☐
ACRFT. TYPE		ACRFT. ID / FLT #	_____ I _____		
ETE (Est. Flight Time)		DEPART. TIME (Zulu)			

ROUTE / WAYPOINTS	WIND	WX
>		
>	____ / ___	
>		

DEPARTURE

GATE / RUNWAY		PAYLOAD		ATC INSTRUCTIONS
ALTIMETER		RESERVE		>
CLIMB RATE		QNH		>
TRANS ALT		SID		>
ZFW		SQUAWK		>
TOW		ATIS INFO		>
BLOCK FUEL		>		>
TAXIWAYS > RNW				>

TAKE OFF / CLIMB / CRUISE PHASE

V_1:	V_R:	V_2:

EST. TOP OF CLIMB	ATC ACTUAL TOP OF CLIMB
>	>

EST. CRUISE FLIGHT LEVEL	ATC ACTUAL CRUISE FLIGHT LEVEL
>	>

DESCENT PHASE / APPROACH

TOP OF DESCENT	TRANSITION ALTITUDE
>	>

STAR		FIELD ELEVATION		Remarks
QNH		MAG / WIND		>
ATIS INFO				

GO AROUND (ALT / HDG / WAYPOINT)	>	

RNW / GATE		V_{APP} (Approach Speed) :	V_{REF} (Landing Speed) :
TAXIWAYS > GATE		>	>

DEPARTURE ⌄	COMMS	ARRIVAL ⌄
GROUND	REMARKS / NOTES	GROUND
TOWER		TOWER
CLEARANCE		APPROACH
CONTROL		CONTROL
RADAR		ILS
ATIS / INFO		ATIS / INFO
VATSIM		VATSIM
IVAO		IVAO

ADDITIONAL INFORMATION

SKECTH

NOTES

ADDITIONAL INFORMATION

SKECTCH

NOTES

DATE: _____

FLIGHT INFORMATIONS

FROM		TO		VFR		IFR	
ACRFT. TYPE		ACRFT. ID / FLT #	_____ I _____	☐		☐	
ETE *(Est. Flight Time)*		DEPART. TIME *(Zulu)*					

ROUTE / WAYPOINTS	WIND	WX
> > >	____ / ____	

DEPARTURE

GATE / RUNWAY		PAYLOAD		**ATC INSTRUCTIONS**
ALTIMETER		RESERVE		>
CLIMB RATE		QNH		>
TRANS ALT		SID		>
ZFW		SQUAWK		>
TOW		ATIS INFO		>
BLOCK FUEL		>		>
TAXIWAYS > RNW				>

TAKE OFF / CLIMB / CRUISE PHASE

V_1:	V_R:	V_2:

EST. TOP OF CLIMB	ATC ACTUAL TOP OF CLIMB
>	>

EST. CRUISE FLIGHT LEVEL	ATC ACTUAL CRUISE FLIGHT LEVEL
>	>

DESCENT PHASE / APPROACH

TOP OF DESCENT	TRANSITION ALTITUDE
>	>

STAR		FIELD ELEVATION		*Remarks*
QNH		MAG / WIND		>
ATIS INFO				

GO AROUND *(ALT / HDG / WAYPOINT)*	>	

RNW / GATE		V_{APP} *(Approach Speed)* :	V_{REF} *(Landing Speed)* :
TAXIWAYS > GATE		>	>

DEPARTURE ⌄		**COMMS**	*ARRIVAL* ⌄	
GROUND		**REMARKS / NOTES**	GROUND	
TOWER			TOWER	
CLEARANCE			APPROACH	
CONTROL			CONTROL	
RADAR			ILS	
ATIS / INFO			ATIS / INFO	
VATSIM			VATSIM	
IVAO			IVAO	

ADDITIONAL INFORMATION

SKECTCH

NOTES

DATE: _____

FLIGHT INFORMATIONS

FROM		TO		VFR		IFR	
ACRFT. TYPE		ACRFT. ID / FLT #	_____ I _____	☐		☐	
ETE *(Est. Flight Time)*		DEPART. TIME *(Zulu)*					

ROUTE / WAYPOINTS	WIND	WX
>	_____ / _____	
>		
>		

DEPARTURE

GATE / RUNWAY		PAYLOAD		ATC INSTRUCTIONS
ALTIMETER		RESERVE		>
CLIMB RATE		QNH		>
TRANS ALT		SID		>
ZFW		SQUAWK		>
TOW		ATIS INFO		>
BLOCK FUEL		>		>
TAXIWAYS > RNW				>

TAKE OFF / CLIMB / CRUISE PHASE

V_1:	V_R:	V_2:

EST. TOP OF CLIMB	ATC ACTUAL TOP OF CLIMB
>	>

EST. CRUISE FLIGHT LEVEL	ATC ACTUAL CRUISE FLIGHT LEVEL
>	>

DESCENT PHASE / APPROACH

TOP OF DESCENT	TRANSITION ALTITUDE
>	>

STAR		FIELD ELEVATION		*Remarks*
QNH		MAG / WIND		>
ATIS INFO				

GO AROUND *(ALT / HDG / WAYPOINT)*	>	

RNW / GATE		V_{APP} *(Approach Speed)* :	V_{REF} *(Landing Speed)* :
TAXIWAYS > GATE		>	>

DEPARTURE		⌄	COMMS	ARRIVAL		⌄
GROUND			**REMARKS / NOTES**	GROUND		
TOWER				TOWER		
CLEARANCE				APPROACH		
CONTROL				CONTROL		
RADAR				ILS		
ATIS / INFO				ATIS / INFO		
VATSIM				VATSIM		
IVAO				IVAO		

ADDITIONAL INFORMATION

SKECTCH

NOTES

DATE: _____

FLIGHT INFORMATIONS

FROM		TO		VFR		IFR	
ACRFT. TYPE		ACRFT. ID / FLT #	_____ I _____	☐		☐	
ETE *(Est. Flight Time)*		DEPART. TIME *(Zulu)*					

ROUTE / WAYPOINTS	WIND	WX
> > >	____ / ____	

DEPARTURE

GATE / RUNWAY		PAYLOAD		ATC INSTRUCTIONS	
ALTIMETER		RESERVE		>	
CLIMB RATE		QNH		>	
TRANS ALT		SID		>	
ZFW		SQUAWK		>	
TOW		ATIS INFO		>	
BLOCK FUEL		>		>	
TAXIWAYS > RNW				>	

TAKE OFF / CLIMB / CRUISE PHASE

V_1:	V_R:	V_2:

EST. TOP OF CLIMB	ATC ACTUAL TOP OF CLIMB
>	>

EST. CRUISE FLIGHT LEVEL	ATC ACTUAL CRUISE FLIGHT LEVEL
>	>

DESCENT PHASE / APPROACH

TOP OF DESCENT	TRANSITION ALTITUDE
>	>

STAR		FIELD ELEVATION		*Remarks*
QNH		MAG / WIND		>
ATIS INFO				

GO AROUND *(ALT / HDG / WAYPOINT)*	>	

RNW / GATE		V_{APP} *(Approach Speed)* :	V_{REF} *(Landing Speed)* :
TAXIWAYS > GATE		>	>

DEPARTURE ⌄	COMMS	*ARRIVAL* ⌄

DEPARTURE		REMARKS / NOTES	ARRIVAL	
GROUND			GROUND	
TOWER			TOWER	
CLEARANCE			APPROACH	
CONTROL			CONTROL	
RADAR			ILS	
ATIS / INFO			ATIS / INFO	
VATSIM			VATSIM	
IVAO			IVAO	

ADDITIONAL INFORMATION

SKECTCH

NOTES

DATE: _____

FLIGHT INFORMATIONS

FROM		TO		VFR	IFR
ACRFT. TYPE		ACRFT. ID / FLT #	_____ I _____	☐	☐
ETE (Est. Flight Time)		DEPART. TIME (Zulu)			

ROUTE / WAYPOINTS	WIND	WX
>		
>	____ / ____	
>		

DEPARTURE

GATE / RUNWAY		PAYLOAD		ATC INSTRUCTIONS
ALTIMETER		RESERVE		>
CLIMB RATE		QNH		>
TRANS ALT		SID		>
ZFW		SQUAWK		>
TOW		ATIS INFO		>
BLOCK FUEL		>		>
TAXIWAYS > RNW				>

TAKE OFF / CLIMB / CRUISE PHASE

V_1:	V_R:	V_2:

EST. TOP OF CLIMB	ATC ACTUAL TOP OF CLIMB
>	>

EST. CRUISE FLIGHT LEVEL	ATC ACTUAL CRUISE FLIGHT LEVEL
>	>

DESCENT PHASE / APPROACH

TOP OF DESCENT	TRANSITION ALTITUDE
>	>

STAR		FIELD ELEVATION		Remarks
QNH		MAG / WIND		>
ATIS INFO				

GO AROUND (ALT / HDG / WAYPOINT)	>	

RNW / GATE		V_{APP} (Approach Speed) :	V_{REF} (Landing Speed) :
TAXIWAYS > GATE		>	>

DEPARTURE		⌄	COMMS	ARRIVAL		⌄

DEPARTURE		REMARKS / NOTES	ARRIVAL	
GROUND			GROUND	
TOWER			TOWER	
CLEARANCE			APPROACH	
CONTROL			CONTROL	
RADAR			ILS	
ATIS / INFO			ATIS / INFO	
VATSIM			VATSIM	
IVAO			IVAO	

ADDITIONAL INFORMATION

SKECTCH

NOTES

DATE: _____

FLIGHT INFORMATIONS

FROM		TO		**VFR**	**IFR**
ACRFT. TYPE		ACRFT. ID / FLT #	_____ I _____	☐	☐
ETE *(Est. Flight Time)*		DEPART. TIME *(Zulu)*			

ROUTE / WAYPOINTS	**WIND**	**WX**
>		
>	____ / ___	
>		

DEPARTURE

GATE / RUNWAY		PAYLOAD		**ATC INSTRUCTIONS**
ALTIMETER		RESERVE		>
CLIMB RATE		QNH		>
TRANS ALT		SID		>
ZFW		SQUAWK		>
TOW		ATIS INFO		>
BLOCK FUEL		>		>
TAXIWAYS > RNW				>

TAKE OFF / CLIMB / CRUISE PHASE

V_1:	V_R:	V_2:

EST. TOP OF CLIMB	ATC ACTUAL TOP OF CLIMB
>	>

EST. CRUISE FLIGHT LEVEL	ATC ACTUAL CRUISE FLIGHT LEVEL
>	>

DESCENT PHASE / APPROACH

TOP OF DESCENT	TRANSITION ALTITUDE
>	>

STAR		FIELD ELEVATION		*Remarks*
QNH		MAG / WIND		>
ATIS INFO				

GO AROUND *(ALT / HDG / WAYPOINT)*	>	

RNW / GATE		V_{APP} *(Approach Speed)* :	V_{REF} *(Landing Speed)* :
TAXIWAYS > GATE		>	>

DEPARTURE ⌄		**COMMS**	*ARRIVAL* ⌄	
GROUND		**REMARKS / NOTES**	GROUND	
TOWER			TOWER	
CLEARANCE			APPROACH	
CONTROL			CONTROL	
RADAR			ILS	
ATIS / INFO			ATIS / INFO	
VATSIM			VATSIM	
IVAO			IVAO	

ADDITIONAL INFORMATION

SKECTH

NOTES

DATE: _____

FLIGHT INFORMATIONS

FROM		TO		**VFR**		**IFR**	
ACRFT. TYPE		ACRFT. ID / FLT #	_____ I _____	☐		☐	
ETE *(Est. Flight Time)*		DEPART. TIME *(Zulu)*					

ROUTE / WAYPOINTS	**WIND**	**WX**
>		
>	_____ / ___	
>		

DEPARTURE

GATE / RUNWAY		PAYLOAD		**ATC INSTRUCTIONS**
ALTIMETER		RESERVE		>
CLIMB RATE		QNH		>
TRANS ALT		SID		>
ZFW		SQUAWK		>
TOW		ATIS INFO		>
BLOCK FUEL		>		>
TAXIWAYS > RNW				>

TAKE OFF / CLIMB / CRUISE PHASE

V_1:		V_R:		V_2:	

EST. TOP OF CLIMB	ATC ACTUAL TOP OF CLIMB
>	>

EST. CRUISE FLIGHT LEVEL	ATC ACTUAL CRUISE FLIGHT LEVEL
>	>

DESCENT PHASE / APPROACH

TOP OF DESCENT	TRANSITION ALTITUDE
>	>

STAR		FIELD ELEVATION		*Remarks*
QNH		MAG / WIND		>
ATIS INFO				

GO AROUND *(ALT / HDG / WAYPOINT)*	>	

RNW / GATE		V_{APP} *(Approach Speed)* :	V_{REF} *(Landing Speed)* :
TAXIWAYS > GATE		>	>

DEPARTURE ⌄		**COMMS**	*ARRIVAL* ⌄	
GROUND		**REMARKS / NOTES**	GROUND	
TOWER			TOWER	
CLEARANCE			APPROACH	
CONTROL			CONTROL	
RADAR			ILS	
ATIS / INFO			ATIS / INFO	
VATSIM			VATSIM	
IVAO			IVAO	

ADDITIONAL INFORMATION

SKECTH

NOTES

DATE: _____

FLIGHT INFORMATIONS

FROM		TO		**VFR**	**IFR**
ACRFT. TYPE		ACRFT. ID / FLT #	_____ I_____	☐	☐
ETE *(Est. Flight Time)*		DEPART. TIME *(Zulu)*			

ROUTE / WAYPOINTS		**WIND** ___ / ___	**WX**
>			
>			
>			

DEPARTURE

GATE / RUNWAY		PAYLOAD		**ATC INSTRUCTIONS**
ALTIMETER		RESERVE		>
CLIMB RATE		QNH		>
TRANS ALT		SID		>
ZFW		SQUAWK		>
TOW		ATIS INFO		>
BLOCK FUEL		>		>
TAXIWAYS > RNW				>

TAKE OFF / CLIMB / CRUISE PHASE

V_1:	V_R:	V_2:

EST. TOP OF CLIMB	**ATC ACTUAL TOP OF CLIMB**
>	>

EST. CRUISE FLIGHT LEVEL	**ATC ACTUAL CRUISE FLIGHT LEVEL**
>	>

DESCENT PHASE / APPROACH

TOP OF DESCENT	TRANSITION ALTITUDE
>	>

STAR		FIELD ELEVATION		*Remarks*
QNH		MAG / WIND		>
ATIS INFO				

GO AROUND *(ALT / HDG / WAYPOINT)*	>	

RNW / GATE		V_{APP} *(Approach Speed)* :	V_{REF} *(Landing Speed)* :
TAXIWAYS > GATE		>	>

DEPARTURE ⌄		**COMMS**	**ARRIVAL** ⌄	
GROUND		**REMARKS / NOTES**	GROUND	
TOWER			TOWER	
CLEARANCE			APPROACH	
CONTROL			CONTROL	
RADAR			ILS	
ATIS / INFO			ATIS / INFO	
VATSIM			VATSIM	
IVAO			IVAO	

ADDITIONAL INFORMATION

SKETCH

NOTES

DATE: _____

FLIGHT INFORMATIONS

FROM		TO		VFR ☐	IFR ☐
ACRFT. TYPE		ACRFT. ID / FLT #	_____ I _____		
ETE (Est. Flight Time)		DEPART. TIME (Zulu)			

ROUTE / WAYPOINTS	WIND ____ / ___	WX
>		
>		
>		

DEPARTURE

GATE / RUNWAY		PAYLOAD		ATC INSTRUCTIONS
ALTIMETER		RESERVE		>
CLIMB RATE		QNH		>
TRANS ALT		SID		>
ZFW		SQUAWK		>
TOW		ATIS INFO		>
BLOCK FUEL		>		>
TAXIWAYS > RNW				>

TAKE OFF / CLIMB / CRUISE PHASE

V_1:	V_R:	V_2:

EST. TOP OF CLIMB	ATC ACTUAL TOP OF CLIMB
>	>

EST. CRUISE FLIGHT LEVEL	ATC ACTUAL CRUISE FLIGHT LEVEL
>	>

DESCENT PHASE / APPROACH

TOP OF DESCENT	TRANSITION ALTITUDE
>	>

STAR		FIELD ELEVATION		Remarks
QNH		MAG / WIND		>
ATIS INFO				

GO AROUND (ALT / HDG / WAYPOINT)	>	

RNW / GATE		V_{APP} (Approach Speed):	V_{REF} (Landing Speed):
TAXIWAYS > GATE		>	>

DEPARTURE ⌄		COMMS	ARRIVAL ⌄	
		REMARKS / NOTES		
GROUND			GROUND	
TOWER			TOWER	
CLEARANCE			APPROACH	
CONTROL			CONTROL	
RADAR			ILS	
ATIS / INFO			ATIS / INFO	
VATSIM			VATSIM	
IVAO			IVAO	

ADDITIONAL INFORMATION

SKECTH

NOTES

DATE: _____

FLIGHT INFORMATIONS

FROM		TO		VFR		IFR	
ACRFT. TYPE		ACRFT. ID / FLT #	_____ I_____	☐		☐	
ETE *(Est. Flight Time)*		DEPART. TIME *(Zulu)*					

ROUTE / WAYPOINTS	WIND	WX
> > >	____ / ____	

DEPARTURE

GATE / RUNWAY		PAYLOAD		ATC INSTRUCTIONS
ALTIMETER		RESERVE		>
CLIMB RATE		QNH		>
TRANS ALT		SID		>
ZFW		SQUAWK		>
TOW		ATIS INFO		>
BLOCK FUEL		>		>
TAXIWAYS > RNW				>

TAKE OFF / CLIMB / CRUISE PHASE

V_1:	V_R:	V_2:

EST. TOP OF CLIMB	ATC ACTUAL TOP OF CLIMB
>	>

EST. CRUISE FLIGHT LEVEL	ATC ACTUAL CRUISE FLIGHT LEVEL
>	>

DESCENT PHASE / APPROACH

TOP OF DESCENT	TRANSITION ALTITUDE
>	>

STAR		FIELD ELEVATION		Remarks
QNH		MAG / WIND		>
ATIS INFO				

GO AROUND *(ALT / HDG / WAYPOINT)*	>	

RNW / GATE		V_{APP} *(Approach Speed)* :	V_{REF} *(Landing Speed)* :
TAXIWAYS > GATE		>	>

DEPARTURE 〰 ∨	COMMS	ARRIVAL 〰 ∨
GROUND	REMARKS / NOTES	GROUND
TOWER		TOWER
CLEARANCE		APPROACH
CONTROL		CONTROL
RADAR		ILS
ATIS / INFO		ATIS / INFO
VATSIM		VATSIM
IVAO		IVAO

ADDITIONAL INFORMATION

SKETCH

NOTES

DATE: _____

FLIGHT INFORMATIONS

FROM		TO		VFR	IFR
ACRFT. TYPE		ACRFT. ID / FLT #	_____ I _____	☐	☐
ETE *(Est. Flight Time)*		DEPART. TIME *(Zulu)*			

ROUTE / WAYPOINTS	WIND	WX
>		
>	_____ / _____	
>		

DEPARTURE

GATE / RUNWAY		PAYLOAD		ATC INSTRUCTIONS	
ALTIMETER		RESERVE		>	
CLIMB RATE		QNH		>	
TRANS ALT		SID		>	
ZFW		SQUAWK		>	
TOW		ATIS INFO		>	
BLOCK FUEL		>		>	
TAXIWAYS > RNW				>	

TAKE OFF / CLIMB / CRUISE PHASE

V_1:		V_R:		V_2:

EST. TOP OF CLIMB	ATC ACTUAL TOP OF CLIMB
>	>

EST. CRUISE FLIGHT LEVEL	ATC ACTUAL CRUISE FLIGHT LEVEL
>	>

DESCENT PHASE / APPROACH

TOP OF DESCENT	TRANSITION ALTITUDE
>	>

STAR		FIELD ELEVATION		Remarks
QNH		MAG / WIND		>
ATIS INFO				

GO AROUND *(ALT / HDG / WAYPOINT)*	>	

RNW / GATE		V_{APP} *(Approach Speed)* :	V_{REF} *(Landing Speed)* :
TAXIWAYS > GATE		>	>

DEPARTURE		∨	COMMS	ARRIVAL		∨
GROUND			REMARKS / NOTES	GROUND		
TOWER				TOWER		
CLEARANCE				APPROACH		
CONTROL				CONTROL		
RADAR				ILS		
ATIS / INFO				ATIS / INFO		
VATSIM				VATSIM		
VAO				IVAO		

ADDITIONAL INFORMATION

SKECTCH

NOTES

DATE: _____

FLIGHT INFORMATIONS

FROM		TO		VFR		IFR	
ACRFT. TYPE		ACRFT. ID / FLT #	_____ I _____	☐		☐	
ETE *(Est. Flight Time)*		DEPART. TIME *(Zulu)*					

ROUTE / WAYPOINTS	WIND	WX
>	____ / ____	
>		
>		

DEPARTURE

GATE / RUNWAY		PAYLOAD		ATC INSTRUCTIONS	
ALTIMETER		RESERVE		>	
CLIMB RATE		QNH		>	
TRANS ALT		SID		>	
ZFW		SQUAWK		>	
TOW		ATIS INFO		>	
BLOCK FUEL		>		>	
TAXIWAYS > RNW				>	

TAKE OFF / CLIMB / CRUISE PHASE

V_1:		V_R:		V_2:	

EST. TOP OF CLIMB	ATC ACTUAL TOP OF CLIMB
>	>

EST. CRUISE FLIGHT LEVEL	ATC ACTUAL CRUISE FLIGHT LEVEL
>	>

DESCENT PHASE / APPROACH

TOP OF DESCENT	TRANSITION ALTITUDE
>	>

STAR		FIELD ELEVATION		Remarks
QNH		MAG / WIND		>
ATIS INFO				

GO AROUND *(ALT / HDG / WAYPOINT)*	>	

RNW / GATE		V_{APP} *(Approach Speed)* :	V_{REF} *(Landing Speed)* :
TAXIWAYS > GATE		>	>

DEPARTURE ⋁	COMMS	*ARRIVAL* ⋁

GROUND		REMARKS / NOTES	GROUND	
TOWER			TOWER	
CLEARANCE			APPROACH	
CONTROL			CONTROL	
RADAR			ILS	
ATIS / INFO			ATIS / INFO	
VATSIM			VATSIM	
IVAO			IVAO	

ADDITIONAL INFORMATION

SKECTH

NOTES

DATE: _____

FLIGHT INFORMATIONS

FROM		TO		VFR	IFR
ACRFT. TYPE		ACRFT. ID / FLT #	_____ I _____	☐	☐
ETE (Est. Flight Time)		DEPART. TIME (Zulu)			

ROUTE / WAYPOINTS	WIND	WX
>	_____ / ____	
>		
>		

DEPARTURE

GATE / RUNWAY		PAYLOAD		ATC INSTRUCTIONS
ALTIMETER		RESERVE		>
CLIMB RATE		QNH		>
TRANS ALT		SID		>
ZFW		SQUAWK		>
TOW		ATIS INFO		>
BLOCK FUEL		>		>
TAXIWAYS > RNW				>

TAKE OFF / CLIMB / CRUISE PHASE

V_1:	V_R:	V_2:

EST. TOP OF CLIMB	ATC ACTUAL TOP OF CLIMB
>	>

EST. CRUISE FLIGHT LEVEL	ATC ACTUAL CRUISE FLIGHT LEVEL
>	>

DESCENT PHASE / APPROACH

TOP OF DESCENT	TRANSITION ALTITUDE
>	>

STAR		FIELD ELEVATION		Remarks
QNH		MAG / WIND		>
ATIS INFO				

GO AROUND (ALT / HDG / WAYPOINT)	>	

RNW / GATE		V_{APP} (Approach Speed):	V_{REF} (Landing Speed):
TAXIWAYS > GATE		>	>

DEPARTURE ⌄		COMMS	ARRIVAL ⌄	
GROUND		REMARKS / NOTES	GROUND	
TOWER			TOWER	
CLEARANCE			APPROACH	
CONTROL			CONTROL	
RADAR			ILS	
ATIS / INFO			ATIS / INFO	
VATSIM			VATSIM	
VAO			IVAO	

ADDITIONAL INFORMATION

SKECTCH

NOTES

DATE: _____

FLIGHT INFORMATIONS

FROM		TO		VFR ☐	IFR ☐
ACRFT. TYPE		ACRFT. ID / FLT #	_____ I _____		
ETE *(Est. Flight Time)*		DEPART. TIME *(Zulu)*			

ROUTE / WAYPOINTS 🗺️	WIND 〜 ____ / ____	WX ☀️⛅☁️🌧️⛈️
>		
>		
>		

DEPARTURE

GATE / RUNWAY		PAYLOAD		ATC INSTRUCTIONS 🎧
ALTIMETER		RESERVE		>
CLIMB RATE		QNH		>
TRANS ALT		SID		>
ZFW		SQUAWK		>
TOW		ATIS INFO		>
BLOCK FUEL		>		>
TAXIWAYS > RNW				>

TAKE OFF / CLIMB / CRUISE PHASE

V_1:	V_R:	V_2:

EST. TOP OF CLIMB	ATC ACTUAL TOP OF CLIMB
>	>

EST. CRUISE FLIGHT LEVEL	ATC ACTUAL CRUISE FLIGHT LEVEL
>	>

DESCENT PHASE / APPROACH

TOP OF DESCENT	TRANSITION ALTITUDE
>	>

STAR		FIELD ELEVATION		*Remarks*
QNH		MAG / WIND		>
ATIS INFO				

GO AROUND *(ALT / HDG / WAYPOINT)* >	

RNW / GATE		V_{APP} *(Approach Speed)* :	V_{REF} *(Landing Speed)* :
TAXIWAYS > GATE		>	>

DEPARTURE 📶 ⌄		COMMS	ARRIVAL 📶 ⌄	
GROUND		**REMARKS / NOTES**	GROUND	
TOWER			TOWER	
CLEARANCE			APPROACH	
CONTROL			CONTROL	
RADAR			ILS	
ATIS / INFO			ATIS / INFO	
VATSIM			VATSIM	
IVAO			IVAO	

ADDITIONAL INFORMATION

SKECTCH

NOTES

DATE: _____

FLIGHT INFORMATIONS

FROM		TO		**VFR** ☐	**IFR** ☐
ACRFT. TYPE		ACRFT. ID / FLT #	___|___		
ETE *(Est. Flight Time)*		DEPART. TIME *(Zulu)*			

ROUTE / WAYPOINTS	**WIND** ___ / ___	**WX**
>		
>		
>		

DEPARTURE

GATE / RUNWAY		PAYLOAD		**ATC INSTRUCTIONS**
ALTIMETER		RESERVE		>
CLIMB RATE		QNH		>
TRANS ALT		SID		>
ZFW		SQUAWK		>
TOW		ATIS INFO		>
BLOCK FUEL		>		>
TAXIWAYS > RNW				>

TAKE OFF / CLIMB / CRUISE PHASE

V_1:	V_R:	V_2:

EST. TOP OF CLIMB	ATC ACTUAL TOP OF CLIMB
>	>

EST. CRUISE FLIGHT LEVEL	ATC ACTUAL CRUISE FLIGHT LEVEL
>	>

DESCENT PHASE / APPROACH

TOP OF DESCENT	TRANSITION ALTITUDE
>	>

STAR		FIELD ELEVATION		*Remarks*
QNH		MAG / WIND		>
ATIS INFO				

GO AROUND *(ALT / HDG / WAYPOINT)*	>	

RNW / GATE		V_{APP} *(Approach Speed)*:	V_{REF} *(Landing Speed)*:
TAXIWAYS > GATE		>	>

COMMS

DEPARTURE ⌄		**REMARKS / NOTES**	**ARRIVAL** ⌄	
GROUND			GROUND	
TOWER			TOWER	
CLEARANCE			APPROACH	
CONTROL			CONTROL	
RADAR			ILS	
ATIS / INFO			ATIS / INFO	
VATSIM			VATSIM	
IVAO			IVAO	

ADDITIONAL INFORMATION

SKETCH

NOTES

DATE: _____

FLIGHT INFORMATIONS

FROM		TO		VFR		IFR	
ACRFT. TYPE		ACRFT. ID / FLT #	_____ I _____	☐		☐	
ETE (Est. Flight Time)		DEPART. TIME (Zulu)					

ROUTE / WAYPOINTS	WIND ____ / ____	WX
>		
>		
>		

DEPARTURE

GATE / RUNWAY		PAYLOAD		ATC INSTRUCTIONS	
ALTIMETER		RESERVE		>	
CLIMB RATE		QNH		>	
TRANS ALT		SID		>	
ZFW		SQUAWK		>	
TOW		ATIS INFO		>	
BLOCK FUEL		>		>	
TAXIWAYS > RNW				>	

TAKE OFF / CLIMB / CRUISE PHASE

V_1:	V_R:	V_2:

EST. TOP OF CLIMB	ATC ACTUAL TOP OF CLIMB
>	>

EST. CRUISE FLIGHT LEVEL	ATC ACTUAL CRUISE FLIGHT LEVEL
>	>

DESCENT PHASE / APPROACH

TOP OF DESCENT	TRANSITION ALTITUDE
>	>

STAR		FIELD ELEVATION		Remarks
QNH		MAG / WIND		>
ATIS INFO				

GO AROUND (ALT / HDG / WAYPOINT)	>	

RNW / GATE		V_{APP} (Approach Speed):	V_{REF} (Landing Speed):
TAXIWAYS > GATE		>	>

DEPARTURE ⌄		COMMS	ARRIVAL ⌄	
GROUND		REMARKS / NOTES	GROUND	
TOWER			TOWER	
CLEARANCE			APPROACH	
CONTROL			CONTROL	
RADAR			ILS	
ATIS / INFO			ATIS / INFO	
VATSIM			VATSIM	
IVAO			IVAO	

ADDITIONAL INFORMATION

SKECTH

NOTES

DATE: _____

FLIGHT INFORMATIONS

FROM		TO		VFR ☐	IFR ☐
ACRFT. TYPE		ACRFT. ID / FLT #	_____ I _____		
ETE *(Est. Flight Time)*		DEPART. TIME *(Zulu)*			

ROUTE / WAYPOINTS 🗺️	WIND 〰️ ____ / ____	WX ☀️⛅☁️🌧️⛈️
>		
>		
>		

DEPARTURE

GATE / RUNWAY		PAYLOAD		ATC INSTRUCTIONS	
ALTIMETER		RESERVE		>	🎧
CLIMB RATE		QNH		>	
TRANS ALT		SID		>	
ZFW		SQUAWK		>	
TOW		ATIS INFO		>	
BLOCK FUEL		>		>	
TAXIWAYS > RNW				>	

TAKE OFF / CLIMB / CRUISE PHASE

V₁:	VR:	V₂:

EST. TOP OF CLIMB	ATC ACTUAL TOP OF CLIMB
>	>
EST. CRUISE FLIGHT LEVEL	ATC ACTUAL CRUISE FLIGHT LEVEL
>	>

DESCENT PHASE / APPROACH

TOP OF DESCENT	TRANSITION ALTITUDE
>	>

STAR		FIELD ELEVATION		Remarks
QNH		MAG / WIND		>
ATIS INFO				

GO AROUND *(ALT / HDG / WAYPOINT)* >	

RNW / GATE		VAPP *(Approach Speed)*:	VREF *(Landing Speed)*:
TAXIWAYS > GATE		>	>

DEPARTURE 📶 ˅	COMMS	ARRIVAL 📶 ˅
	REMARKS / NOTES	

DEPARTURE			ARRIVAL	
GROUND			GROUND	
TOWER			TOWER	
CLEARANCE			APPROACH	
CONTROL			CONTROL	
RADAR			ILS	
ATIS / INFO			ATIS / INFO	
VATSIM			VATSIM	
IVAO			IVAO	

ADDITIONAL INFORMATION

SKECTCH

NOTES

DATE: _____

FLIGHT INFORMATIONS

FROM		TO		VFR	IFR
ACRFT. TYPE		ACRFT. ID / FLT #	_____	_____	☐	☐
ETE *(Est. Flight Time)*		DEPART. TIME *(Zulu)*			

ROUTE / WAYPOINTS	WIND	WX
>	_____ / _____	
>		
>		

DEPARTURE

GATE / RUNWAY		PAYLOAD		ATC INSTRUCTIONS	
ALTIMETER		RESERVE		>	
CLIMB RATE		QNH		>	
TRANS ALT		SID		>	
ZFW		SQUAWK		>	
TOW		ATIS INFO		>	
BLOCK FUEL		>		>	
TAXIWAYS > RNW				>	

TAKE OFF / CLIMB / CRUISE PHASE

V_1:	V_R:	V_2:

EST. TOP OF CLIMB	ATC ACTUAL TOP OF CLIMB
>	>

EST. CRUISE FLIGHT LEVEL	ATC ACTUAL CRUISE FLIGHT LEVEL
>	>

DESCENT PHASE / APPROACH

TOP OF DESCENT	TRANSITION ALTITUDE
>	>

STAR		FIELD ELEVATION		*Remarks*
QNH		MAG / WIND		>
ATIS INFO				

GO AROUND *(ALT / HDG / WAYPOINT)*	>	

RNW / GATE		V_{APP} *(Approach Speed)* :	V_{REF} *(Landing Speed)* :
TAXIWAYS > GATE		>	>

DEPARTURE ⌄	COMMS	*ARRIVAL* ⌄	
GROUND		REMARKS / NOTES	GROUND	
TOWER			TOWER	
CLEARANCE			APPROACH	
CONTROL			CONTROL	
RADAR			ILS	
ATIS / INFO			ATIS / INFO	
VATSIM			VATSIM	
IVAO			IVAO	

ADDITIONAL INFORMATION

SKECTH

NOTES

DATE: _____

FLIGHT INFORMATIONS

FROM		TO		**VFR** ☐	**IFR** ☐
ACRFT. TYPE		ACRFT. ID / FLT #	_____ l _____		
ETE *(Est. Flight Time)*		DEPART. TIME *(Zulu)*			

ROUTE / WAYPOINTS 🗺️	**WIND** 〰️ ____ / ____	**WX** ☀️🌤️☁️🌧️⛈️
>		
>		
>		

DEPARTURE

GATE / RUNWAY		PAYLOAD		**ATC INSTRUCTIONS** 🎧
ALTIMETER		RESERVE		>
CLIMB RATE		QNH		>
TRANS ALT		SID		>
ZFW		SQUAWK		>
TOW		ATIS INFO		>
BLOCK FUEL		>		>
TAXIWAYS > RNW				>

TAKE OFF / CLIMB / CRUISE PHASE

V_1:	V_R:	V_2:

EST. TOP OF CLIMB	ATC ACTUAL TOP OF CLIMB
>	>

EST. CRUISE FLIGHT LEVEL	ATC ACTUAL CRUISE FLIGHT LEVEL
>	>

DESCENT PHASE / APPROACH

TOP OF DESCENT	TRANSITION ALTITUDE
>	>

STAR		FIELD ELEVATION		*Remarks*
QNH		MAG / WIND		>
ATIS INFO				

GO AROUND *(ALT / HDG / WAYPOINT)* >	

RNW / GATE		V_{APP} *(Approach Speed)* :	V_{REF} *(Landing Speed)* :
TAXIWAYS > GATE		>	>

COMMS

DEPARTURE 📡 ˅		**REMARKS / NOTES**	*ARRIVAL* 📡 ˅	
GROUND			GROUND	
TOWER			TOWER	
CLEARANCE			APPROACH	
CONTROL			CONTROL	
RADAR			ILS	
ATIS / INFO			ATIS / INFO	
VATSIM			VATSIM	
IVAO			IVAO	

ADDITIONAL INFORMATION

SKETCH

NOTES

DATE: _____

FLIGHT INFORMATIONS

FROM		TO		VFR		IFR	
ACRFT. TYPE		ACRFT. ID / FLT #	_____ I _____	☐		☐	
ETE *(Est. Flight Time)*		DEPART. TIME *(Zulu)*					

ROUTE / WAYPOINTS	WIND	WX
> > >	_____ / ____	

DEPARTURE

GATE / RUNWAY		PAYLOAD		ATC INSTRUCTIONS	
ALTIMETER		RESERVE		>	
CLIMB RATE		QNH		>	
TRANS ALT		SID		>	
ZFW		SQUAWK		>	
TOW		ATIS INFO		>	
BLOCK FUEL		>		>	
TAXIWAYS > RNW				>	

TAKE OFF / CLIMB / CRUISE PHASE

V_1:	V_R:	V_2:

EST. TOP OF CLIMB	ATC ACTUAL TOP OF CLIMB
>	>

EST. CRUISE FLIGHT LEVEL	ATC ACTUAL CRUISE FLIGHT LEVEL
>	>

DESCENT PHASE / APPROACH

TOP OF DESCENT	TRANSITION ALTITUDE
>	>

STAR		FIELD ELEVATION		*Remarks*
QNH		MAG / WIND		>
ATIS INFO				

GO AROUND *(ALT / HDG / WAYPOINT)*	>	

RNW / GATE		V_{APP} *(Approach Speed)* :	V_{REF} *(Landing Speed)* :
TAXIWAYS > GATE		>	>

DEPARTURE ∨		COMMS	*ARRIVAL* ∨	
GROUND		REMARKS / NOTES	GROUND	
TOWER			TOWER	
CLEARANCE			APPROACH	
CONTROL			CONTROL	
RADAR			ILS	
ATIS / INFO			ATIS / INFO	
VATSIM			VATSIM	
IVAO			IVAO	

ADDITIONAL INFORMATION

SKECTCH

NOTES

DATE: _____

FLIGHT INFORMATIONS

FROM		TO		VFR	IFR
ACRFT. TYPE		ACRFT. ID / FLT #	_____ I _____	☐	☐
ETE *(Est. Flight Time)*		DEPART. TIME *(Zulu)*			

ROUTE / WAYPOINTS	WIND	WX
> > >	____ / ____	

DEPARTURE

GATE / RUNWAY		PAYLOAD		ATC INSTRUCTIONS
ALTIMETER		RESERVE		>
CLIMB RATE		QNH		>
TRANS ALT		SID		>
ZFW		SQUAWK		>
TOW		ATIS INFO		>
BLOCK FUEL		>		>
TAXIWAYS > RNW				>

TAKE OFF / CLIMB / CRUISE PHASE

V_1:	V_R:	V_2:

EST. TOP OF CLIMB	ATC ACTUAL TOP OF CLIMB
>	>

EST. CRUISE FLIGHT LEVEL	ATC ACTUAL CRUISE FLIGHT LEVEL
>	>

DESCENT PHASE / APPROACH

TOP OF DESCENT	TRANSITION ALTITUDE
>	>

STAR		FIELD ELEVATION		*Remarks*
QNH		MAG / WIND		>
ATIS INFO				

GO AROUND *(ALT / HDG / WAYPOINT)*	>	

RNW / GATE		V_{APP} *(Approach Speed)*:	V_{REF} *(Landing Speed)*:
TAXIWAYS > GATE		>	>

DEPARTURE ⌄	COMMS	*ARRIVAL* ⌄

DEPARTURE		REMARKS / NOTES	ARRIVAL	
GROUND			GROUND	
TOWER			TOWER	
CLEARANCE			APPROACH	
CONTROL			CONTROL	
RADAR			ILS	
ATIS / INFO			ATIS / INFO	
VATSIM			VATSIM	
IVAO			IVAO	

ADDITIONAL INFORMATION

SKECTCH

NOTES

DATE: _____

FLIGHT INFORMATIONS

FROM		TO		**VFR**		**IFR**	
ACRFT. TYPE		ACRFT. ID / FLT #	_____ I _____	☐		☐	
ETE *(Est. Flight Time)*		DEPART. TIME *(Zulu)*					

ROUTE / WAYPOINTS	**WIND**	**WX**
>		
>	____ / ____	
>		

DEPARTURE

GATE / RUNWAY		PAYLOAD		**ATC INSTRUCTIONS**
ALTIMETER		RESERVE		>
CLIMB RATE		QNH		>
TRANS ALT		SID		>
ZFW		SQUAWK		>
TOW		ATIS INFO		>
BLOCK FUEL		>		>
TAXIWAYS > RNW				>

TAKE OFF / CLIMB / CRUISE PHASE

V_1:	V_R:	V_2:

EST. TOP OF CLIMB	ATC ACTUAL TOP OF CLIMB
>	>

EST. CRUISE FLIGHT LEVEL	ATC ACTUAL CRUISE FLIGHT LEVEL
>	>

DESCENT PHASE / APPROACH

TOP OF DESCENT	TRANSITION ALTITUDE
>	>

STAR		FIELD ELEVATION		*Remarks*
QNH		MAG / WIND		>
ATIS INFO				

GO AROUND *(ALT / HDG / WAYPOINT)* >	

RNW / GATE		V_{APP} *(Approach Speed)* :	V_{REF} *(Landing Speed)* :
TAXIWAYS > GATE		>	>

DEPARTURE		∨	**COMMS**	*ARRIVAL*		∨
GROUND			**REMARKS / NOTES**	GROUND		
TOWER				TOWER		
CLEARANCE				APPROACH		
CONTROL				CONTROL		
RADAR				ILS		
ATIS / INFO				ATIS / INFO		
VATSIM				VATSIM		
IVAO				IVAO		

ADDITIONAL INFORMATION

SKECTCH

NOTES

WE HOPE YOU HAD A GREAT TIME!

If you enjoyed this notebook and found it useful for you as a virtual pilot, please be kind as to **leave us your positive review on Amazon,** and like many other users, feel free to post your best pictures of this book.

PILOT LOGBOOK FOR SIMMERS: The Perfect and Handy Flight Simulator Handbook...

Frederic Gosset

★★★★⯨ 28

Paperback

$9.99 ✓prime

 Cody Jackson

☆☆☆☆☆ **Amazing will definitely fill this up and be back for more**

Reviewed in the United States on December 25, 2020

Just got this for Christmas after talking to the author and this is amazing if your remotely serious about flight sims

KRIS DADDY

☆☆☆☆☆ **Pratique et de Qualité**

Reviewed in France on January 6, 2021

Verified Purchase

Tres beau produit en terme de qualité papier de la couverture au livret.
Bien pensé pour flight simmer.
J'ose même pas écrire dessus pour ne pas raturer lol

 Kindle Customer

☆☆☆☆☆ **Flight log**

Reviewed in the United Kingdo

Verified Purchase

Had everything I needed

Luis V.

☆☆☆☆☆ **Muy util**

Reviewed in Mexico on February 7, 2021

Verified Purchase

Excelente producto, lo recomiendo mucho!

Standard Edition

Deluxe Edition

From the same Author... Available on Amazon!